FOURTH GOSPEL

DISCOURSES

**BY
JOHN S RUSSELL**

This booklet is copyright and may not be copied or reproduced, in whole or in part, by any means, without the publisher's prior written consent.

© Copyright 1995
Printed 1996

Abacus Educational Services
424 Birmingham Road, Marlbrook
Bromsgrove, Worcestershire
B61 0HL

ISBN 1 898653 12 7

Other titles available:

Synoptic Gospels series
   1. Source Criticism
   2. Form Criticism
   3. Redaction Criticism
   4. Kingdom of God

Fourth Gospel series
   1. Signs
   2. Eschatology and Judgement
   3. Holy Spirit

Philosophy of Religion series
   1. Religious Language
   2. Problem of Evil
   3. Faith and Reason
   5. Revelation & Religious Experience

Other titles in preparation:

Fourth Gospel series
   5. Prologue

Philosophy of Religion series
   4. Proof and God
   6. Life after Death
   7. Miracles

CONTENTS

INTRODUCTION	4
WHAT IS A DISCOURSE?	5
'I AM' SAYINGS:	
Comments on 'I am'	7
7 'I am' sayings	9
Bread of Life	10
Light of the world	13
Door of the sheep	20
Good Shepherd	23
Resurrection and Life	27
Way, Truth and Life	32
True Vine	37
OTHER DISCOURSES (Non 'I am' sayings):	
Nicodemus	43
Samaritan woman	45
After healing of crippled man	50
Tabernacles	52
When Greeks arrive	55
Final discourse	56
Brief comments on SOURCES, HISTORICITY AND PURPOSES	58
WORKSHEET	60
EXAM QUESTIONS	61
FURTHER READING	63

INTRODUCTION

This series of booklets has been written specifically to cater for the needs of A/AS students of Religious Studies. However, it may equally be used as an introduction to areas of John's Gospel by the interested lay person or by first year undergraduates, especially those at Theological College.

The style of this booklet is similar to those in the series on the Synoptic Gospels, containing consideration of the topic's main features, a worksheet and a section on examination questions, making the booklet useful for both teaching and revision.

Reference has been made to the works of 'scholars' to indicate (rather than fully discuss) the scope of their ideas on the topic and to show the value of many views in answering examination questions.

Highlighting in bold has been used to indicate certain points within paragraphs and to make it easier to follow the points being made.

Further booklets in this series are being produced and together they will supplement the already successful series on the Synoptic Gospels (by R. Addis, P. Cole and J. Lee).

WHAT IS A 'DISCOURSE'?

The term discourse seems to have a rather diverse meaning as can be seen when one looks at any general dictionary definition. A discourse may simply be a talk yet the talk could be a short address or even a lecture. More generally a conversation may be thought of, suggesting the involvement of more then one person, or even, when considering 'religious' discourse, a sermon might be intended.

Certainly when considering the **Fourth Gospel** the term discourse may be seen as an **'umbrella' term**; this seems confirmed by the way certain scholars use 'discourse' to describe a **variety of communication types.**

Dodd (The Interpretation of the Fourth Gospel), for example, frequently writes of dialogue when considering discourses, though such **dialogue** is described as dramatic dialogue in Chapters 3 and 4 or as sustained dialogue between Jesus and the crowd in Chapter 6. Such sustained elements are also present as long continuous discourse as in Chapters 5 and 10, though these are different from the dialogues or conversations (Barrett 'The Gospel according to St. John', pg12) of Chapters 7 and 8 which are more controversial or are as Smalley ('John: Evangelist and Interpreter', (pg89) writes **'conflict-discourse'.**

Bultmann ('The Gospel of John, pg347) suggests that it is part of a 'Johannine style' to have a discourse where the flow is interrupted by **people 'butting in'**. These people are called 'interlocutors' whose interruptions allow a clarification of intended meaning as the audience takes literally what are meant to be symbolically statements. Barrett (pg208) suggests there emerges a sort of pattern with a statement leading to **misunderstanding** followed by further teaching to 'advance' the ideas being presented. Bultmann (pg4) hints that the initial statement has an intended double meaning; if so it might also be suggested that the intention is to point out that the people merely have a capacity to see superficially rather than grasp the depth of Jesus' real meaning.

A further descriptor used of Johannine discourses is **monologue.** For example, in the Nicodemus passage in Chapter 3 the initial dialogue passes into monologue as Nicodemus seems to disappear leaving Jesus to give his teaching. Dodd when referring to Ch.15v1-16v15 (pg410) writes 'we have pure monologue', or almost pure discourse uninterrupted by questions and answers (Barrett pg14). As a 'rule of thumb' Marsh ('St. John', pg259) mentions that generally when the text has the double amen (in truth, in very truth) the writer is entering the realm of monologue, though sensibly against oversimplification Grayston points out that dialogue and monologue are not always distinguished ('The Gospel of John', pgxviii). Indeed, even though narrative material may be considered as separate from discourse Barrett suggests when referring to Chapters 4, 9 and 11, that 'narrative and discourse are woven together' (pg20).

Scholars also refer to Johannine discourse material as **sermon.** They often indicate that there is a real Johannine participation within the discourse material and that the discourse material may reflect more the sitz im leben of the evangelist or the Johannine church rather than that of Jesus. Thus Barrett (pg21) feels that the hypothesis that discourses were in the first place sermons delivered by the evangelist 'has much to commend it.' Similarly Bultmann (pg4) suggests that John's Gospel 'contains continuous sermons in which occasionally individual and original independent logia may be found firmly extended' which Marsh (pg308) sees as possibly sermon material drawn together by the evangelist around a common theme, as for example in chapter 6 around the theme of Passover.

There is also a suggestion that the **discourses reflect the dialogue between Christians and Jews,** the church and synagogue at the end of the first century. Such material is also referred to as 'debate' through which is 'revealed the sharpest antagonism to the Jews' (Barrett pg334). Moreover it is suggested that this material may be primitive Christian material which the evangelist has deepened and 'sharpened its edge'.

Such comments may lead some to the conclusion that discourse material in John's Gospel may have the least claim to authenticity in terms of Jesus' actual words. However, more conservative scholars such as Hunter ('According to John', pg94) support the possibility that the Johannine discourses are in fact enshrining 'a genuine tradition of an aspect of Jesus' teaching which has not found a place in the Synoptics.'

▶Johannine 'Discourse' passages

When reference is made to the discourses of the Fourth Gospel many people immediately think of the 7 (predicated) 'I am sayings'. However, there are discourses elsewhere in John's Gospel; thus both the 'I am' sayings and the other material will be considered.

'I AM SAYINGS'?

The phrase 'I am' (in Greek **'ego eimi'**) occurs 29 times in John's Gospel, of which 26 times are in the mouth of Jesus (Schnackenburg 'The Gospel according to St. John', pg 79) which causes the scholar to conclude that 'I am' is a "consciously used and theologically significant expression which has become a highly compressed formula". The **background** of the phrase **'I am'** in John's Gospel has been debated. Some scholars suggest a **pagan or Greek/Hellenistic background**. For example, reference is made to the goddess Isis using 'I am', or to the Hermetic Corpus where Poimandres reveals himself to Hermes (eg. Barrett pg292). Howard ('Christianity according to St. John', pg20) agrees that the 'I am' form of speech is the appropriate language of the deity in the Hermetic books but also suggests it is to be found in certain 'magical papyri'.

Many scholars cite the **Old Testament** where 'I am' seems to be the language of the divine as in Deut. 32v39 and Isaiah 43v10. Barrett (pg292) suggests that 'I am' is the divine word of self-revelation and command' and refers to Exodus 3v6, v14 and 20v2, while Grayston (pg62) writes of 'the self assertion of the deity'. Recently Hurtado in 'One God, One Lord' has argued that the Jewish background may not necessarily suggest that 'I am' is identical to God but may be linked with the idea of angels who may 'share' God's name. Moreover links are also made with Wisdom; thus in Proverbs Ch. 8 Wisdom emphasises the Hebrew word for 'I' (elsewhere translated 'I am') in announcing her own virtues.

Brown ('The Gospel according to John', pg535) gives a useful list of ways 'I am' is used to show **different perspectives of God**. For example how God identifies Himself with 'I am Yahweh'; or to assure his people, for because He is 'I am' they need not fear; can trust his statements but will know He is God through His actions. Brown further suggests that 'I am Yahweh' differentiates Yahweh from any other, and that 'I am' may be even used as a name in itself as in the LXX (Greek) translation of Isaiah 43v25 'I am I am'. He also points out that 'I am' may be predicated, with for example such descriptors as 'salvation' (Psalm 35v3) and 'healer' (Exod. 15v26).

Brown also wonders if the **Synoptic Gospels** may provide a background to John's usage of 'I am'. Brown cites three references: firstly, Mk. 14v62 which may mean 'yes', but also more as the son of man will sit at the right hand of God; secondly, Mt. 14v27 where Jesus is 'I am' so they need not fear and in v33 Jesus is acknowledged as God's Son; thirdly, Lk. 24v36 where 'It is I' may be indicated but where the 'I am' may reveal Jesus' lordship. However, it should be noted that there are no 'I am' sayings with the (descriptive) predicate in the Synoptics.

▶John's usage of the term 'I am'

Brown indicates (pg533) that in the Fourth Gospel there are three types of 'I am' sayings. **Firstly, there is the absolute with no predicates** (eg. 8v24, 28, 58 and 13v19). Brown feels these statements almost seem incomplete and so it may not be surprising that in 8v25 the people ask 'Who are you?' even after the 'I am' in v24. **Secondly there are references where there is no expressed predicate but where it may seem understood** (eg 6v20, 18v5, 6, 8). In 6v20 'I am' may seem no more than 'It is I (someone you know) so don't be afraid'. Yet as noted above, in the Old Testament there are divine theophanies (God revealing himself) where the people are told not to fear, so in 6v20 John may be combining the ordinary and 'sacral' use. Similarly in 18v5 when Jesus tells the arresting force 'I am' it may be more than 'I am the one you want' as the people fall to the ground as though in the presence of the divine. **Thirdly, 'I am' is accompanied with a nominative predicate** (eg 6v35 'I am the bread of life' or 9v5 'I am the light of the world'). Barrett (pg291) indicates that this usage was a striking characteristic of John's style. Bultmann (ref. Brown pg534) believes that the emphasis in 6v35 is on the 'I' so as to contrast Jesus with any other person (here with Moses). Thus 'Bread it is I' where 'I' would seem itself a predicate. Brown (pg534) and others question Bultmann's interpretation arguing the emphasis is not solely an emphasis on the person of Jesus himself but also on his role, what he is in relation to men; thus for example he is bread to indicate the nourishment he gives. Schnackenburg (pg88) suggests that while the Old Testament formula 'I am' attributed to Jesus might to Jews give him an unprecedented status, it would be a misunderstanding to interpret Jesus' high claims as an identification with God. This is part of the wider debate on whether or not Jesus' use of the 'divine' phrase means he is himself claiming to be divine. (Note the Person of Jesus will be explored in a future booklet).

▶The 7 (predicated) 'I am' sayings

Some scholars suggest that there may be **significance in John using '7' sayings**, namely to suggest perfection in Jesus' pronouncements. Smalley argues (pgs90-1) that the 7 sayings correlate to the 7 signs, (though in his list he replaces the Walking on the Water with the Catch of Fish (Ch. 21); thus for example, 'I am the true vine' is linked to water to wine and 'I am the good shepherd' to the catch of fish. He further suggests (pgs89-90) that each of the signs is also related to a discourse passage, writing of the "careful way in which John has put together his Gospel, so that each of the seven signs is associated with discourse material which explicates at leisure its real significance and spiritual implications". Morris in 'Jesus Christ' (pg23) also links discourses with signs but his list is different to Smalley's as Morris uses the walking on the water which he links with the chapter 7 discourse; yet readers beware as Morris himself seems to be unsure of the latter's appropriateness as a link, and even Smalley is hesitant in linking the sign of the officer's son with the 'I am the way, the truth, and the life' saying.

In the pages that follow the 7 (predicated) 'I am' sayings will be investigated and certain comments will be made drawing out possible links between the background material and Johannine thought. While it must remain supposition, it is possible that such passages may have had some influence on the way the evangelist of the Fourth Gospel has presented his material; he may have wished to echo passages with which his audience may have been familiar and to relate his beliefs about the person of Jesus in the light of such material.

▶Bread of Life discourse (Ch.6v26-71)

The passage follows the feeding of the 5000, the walking on the water, and the journeying of 'the people' to find Jesus.

From 6v26 much of the material is in the form of a monologue of Jesus but with interjections from 'the Jews' often in terms of disapproval.

The major thrusts of the passage are clearly **Christological** (thus Beasley-Murray 'John', pg86). The evangelist in particular wishes to stress that it is through Jesus that eternal life is made available by believing in him and feeding on his bread. The evangelist repeatedly presents Jesus as **the heavenly bread**; he is the one from above giving his food to believers. The evangelist may be recalling the food/nectar (ambrosia) of the gods in Homer or the food of the angels, the heavenly manna (Psalm 78v25). John constantly alludes in the passage to the **manna of the wilderness** clearly at this point at least recalling Old Testament material. For example in Nehemiah 9v15 it is recalled how God gave manna from heaven in the wilderness and in abundance in Psalm 105v40. Yet in particular Jews would be reminded of Exodus Chapter 16 where the giving of manna by God demonstrated (v12) He was 'I am the Lord your God'. The scholar Borgen in an article 'Bread from heaven' (1965) interestingly argues that v31-58 of the discourse in Chapter 6 represent an extended commentary on the text of Exodus 16v4 'Behold I will rain bread from heaven for you.', though others have wondered if the text being 'commented' on is Psalm 78v24. If either suggestion was correct then the discourse would justifiably be described as a sermon.

Yet John's purpose, and one of his unique touches, is to use this manna to **contrast with 'Bread Jesus'** in order to show the **superiority of Bread Jesus** over any other spiritual or nourishing food. Thus Jesus is the 'real' (true) bread, with its possible Platonic links, for Plato differentiated in his philosophy between the absolute reality and its mere shadows.

The Jews gave great acclaim to Moses for giving the bread from heaven to the wilderness travellers, yet John seems to emphasise that it was not Moses who actually gave their ancestors bread in the wilderness rather it was God. He clearly wishes to **redirect their attention away both from Moses and the past**, including within it the death of their forefathers. Instead they are called upon to focus on Jesus himself who is the true bread that God is 'now' giving to his people, hence Jesus is emphasised in the present tense 'am' (eg v35, 41, 47, 51). He can provide spiritual nourishment which has future consequences in that they can have Jesus' protection and '**life**' for he is not merely bread but bread of that life.

The word **life (Greek 'zoe')** is common in John's Gospel and to bring human beings to that life seems to be a major purpose of his Gospel (20v31). Jesus as the pre-existent Logos was the **bringer of life** to the world at creation, and God granted him power to give that life to all God had given him (17v2) and to give that life abundantly (10v10). 'Life' is often expressed in the characteristically Johannine form of **'eternal life'**. Eternal (Greek 'aionios') is a word of eternity and deity which according to Barclay ('The Gospels and Acts' vol 2, pg 222) 'can only properly be applied to God.' So 'eternal life' implies a life coming from the source that is itself divine and eternal. Yet eternal life means more than just continuing to exist; it strongly expresses the feeling of a relationship. The fourth evangelist seems to define the term in Ch. 17v3 as 'this is eternal life, that they know thee the only true God, and Jesus Christ whom thou hast sent.' Also for the evangelist the dynamic thrust of eternal life is not to show it in terms of the age to come nor in the future at the end of history, but in terms of its availability in the present world. So in Chapter 6 if the people are willing to partake of Jesus' spiritual nourishment they will 'never die'; they must still be willing to eat or else they will not live but rather perish.

For the Jew the Law (Torah) was symbolised by 'bread' and it may be that the evangelist's intention is also to **take his audience's attention off the 'Torah' bread** which they believed would lead to life and which they might also have attributed to (or through) Moses. They are thus challenged to accept God's present offer and eat Bread Jesus, as he is the 'gift' itself (Bultmann pg227), and is the real eternal life bread which seems to **supersede both the Torah and Moses' manna**.

The 'nowness' of the offer also demonstrates the **present reality of the eschatological messianic age** with its banquet associations. For the Jew bread was linked with the messiah though even in the Sibylline Oracles manna was the food of the messianic community. At the feeding of the 5000 the Jews had seemingly recognised Jesus as messiah but clearly only as a political figure whom they might make their 'king'. Jesus had withdrawn from them and turned his back on that political role as messiah and now he tries to draw them to see his spiritual nature and eternal life which can be theirs, as God is now giving 'real bread'. However, while from the opening verses of the discourse Jesus has been trying to turn their **attention from physical to eternal bread**, throughout the discourse the Jews only seem to be pre-occupied with the physical concerns of the bread, the sign, and the fact that they did not know Jesus' parents. Further, and in particular from v53, all that is offered must come through eating his flesh, which, together with his blood, is the real manna (Sanders and Mastin 'The Gospel according to St. John', pg54), though the Jews merely see this as suggesting cannibalism.

This material has been accepted by many as **'eucharistic'**, a view made stronger by the allusions to 'drinking his blood' in v54, 55, and 56, though some (eg Bultmann pg234) argue the material may have been added by a redactor rather the being 'original' Johannine material. Some have suggested that this discourse may be a Johannine interpretation of the Institution of the Eucharist at the Last Supper in the Synoptic Gospels. (The invitation both to eat and drink is also a feature of Isaiah 55v1). While some scholars argue that the discourse is a revelatory teaching of Jesus that is non-eucharistic, others, for example Beasley-Murray (pg98), see within the passage a sacramental metaphor, and that as the discourse progresses there is an increase in the sacramental emphasis (particularly from v51). Indeed Brown (pg272) sees the whole passage as a discourse drawing out the eucharistic significance of the feeding of the 5000 itself. For some this possible 'eucharistic' presence raises the question of historicity of this, and other, discourse material, with the possibility that they are literary constructions of the evangelist and not the words of Jesus.

It has been suggested that the evangelist uses 'bread' to make a **link with Wisdom** echoing for example Provs. 9v5 where Wisdom's invitation is to 'Come, eat of my bread' or in the Rabbinic Sir. 15v3 where Wisdom nourishes with bread. The Wisdom link seems made more likely by Provs. 9v5 also containing 'and drink of the wine I have mixed' with the apparent reflection of John's eating and 'drinking' in 6v54-56.

It also seems worth remembering that bread was connected **with the temple** as the 'temple bread' or 'priests' bread' kept within the Holy

Place; yet for the evangelist Jesus' body is itself the 'temple' (Ch. 2v21) which will be destroyed but rise again. He will give this temple bread (the bread and body of the Last Supper) to those who will merely accept its offer, as he will also provide spiritual refreshment for their thirst. He further makes this offer in chapter 7 when he is himself in their earthly temple and states that they should come to him if they thirst and they will receive 'rivers of living water', interpreted in 7v39 as 'the Spirit'.

Finally, it should be noted that throughout the discourse (and even within the feeding itself) there is some concentration on the **theme of 'believing'**, as though there is a debate in progress leading to a decision on believing or otherwise. Initially, in answer to the Jews' question 'What must we do?' (v28), Jesus indicates that all they need to do to do the works of God is to believe on the one He has sent, though they want some sort of messianic sign to convince them to believe. The believer will be nourished but Jesus acknowledges that though they have seen him they do not believe. Indeed though to believe will 'truly, truly' gain them eternal life the Jews only murmur against his claims, and there are even those of his disciple group who no-longer went around with him, and they have not been called upon to witness such a marvel as the son of man re-ascending to his 'above' realm.

The passage ends with what may be a Johannine version of the 'Petrine confession' (Mk. 8v29). In John's Gospel Peter states that the twelve are staying with Jesus as "we have believed" which has led them to 'know' he is the Holy One of God (a term which some see as an acknowledgement that Jesus is the messiah). However even within that apparent 'inner ring' of believers one of them is a devil for Judas will betray his master; so perhaps even those claiming to be believers should beware for they may move away from him who is 'Life Bread'.

▶ Light of the World discourse (Ch. 9v1-41 and Ch. 8v12-59)

Jesus identifies himself as 'light of the world' first in Ch. 8v12. It seems that it is still the time of the feast of Tabernacles (see also Ch. 7) to which Dodd (pg348) states there are deliberate allusions in Chs. 7 and 8, while Sanders and Mastin (pg218) see Jesus as the true light of the world as linked with the illumination of the Temple at the feast.

However 'light' is not directly alluded to again until Jesus restates he is 'light of the world' in Ch. 9v5. Barrett suggests (pg333) that the statement is made in Ch. 8v12 merely to introduce and raise questions about witness-bearing, with the pronouncement of Jesus about himself allowing the dialogue to be 'set in motion'.

The problem will be tackled by a consideration first of Ch. 9 and then some observations will be made about Ch. 8.

In **Ch. 9** Jesus' comments on light are introduced by his disciples asking the question about a man born blind "who sinned, this man or his parents, that he was born blind?". This reflected the Jewish belief that blindness might be the consequence of sin, though here there is the problem that the man was 'born' blind. Jesus tries to **remove their concerns from sin to 'the works of God'**, here the giving of light, which will be made manifest through the cure of the blind man. Such works are to be done while it is day for night prevents such works being accomplished. Then Jesus pronounces that he himself is that day, that 'light of the world'.

'Light' would be **meaningful to a wide audience**. In **Greek and Roman mysticism** light was identified with God; this is particularly clear in the Hermetic literature. **Philo** talks of 'Lord is my light' and 'First God is light'. In the **Old Testament**, passages such as Psalm 27v1 'The Lord is my light and salvation', or Isaiah 60v19 'the Lord will be your everlasting light' might be recalled. Perhaps more relevant to this Johannine passage would seem God's **creation of light in Genesis Ch. 1**, for Jesus' healing by spitting on the ground to make clay and anointing the man's eyes with it has been seen by some as related to the creation of Adam again in Genesis 1. Here Jesus issues the word to the man that he should 'Go wash in the pool of Siloam'. The man goes, washes and returns 'seeing'. The evangelist indicates that Siloam meant 'sent' and seems thereby to link the pool with Jesus who is repeatedly spoken of by John as the one 'sent' by God. Thus the man is washed in Christ and thereby **enlightened**.

It may be that the 'washing' here is sacramental, that is it alludes to **baptism**, and is an encouragement of that sacred rite to the Gospel's readers. The discourse itself could be a baptismal sermon which reflects on Jesus and the nature of his activity, which while it may cause opposition, may lead some to the almost creedal statement of the now seeing man in v38 'Lord I believe.'

After v7 we hear nothing further from Jesus until the climax of the passage in v39-41. Instead **the man** now cured of blindness **becomes the centre of the 'investigations'** of the Jewish authorities, though the evangelist creates a series of dialogues between various people which leads us to that climax. Thus, the Jews question whether the man is the one who they had seen as a blind man begging; the man confirms he is 'the man', and tells them of his cure by Jesus. Then the 'investigations' really get under way. Indeed **the man seems** to be put **almost on trial** for being cured with the Pharisees emerging as his prosecutors. They even try to involve his parents. However, the 'interrogation' serves a deeper purpose than a trial of the man for at the centre of the questions is in fact the person of Jesus. For while Jesus has earlier encouraged his disciples not to concentrate on 'sin' but on the glorious works of God, the Pharisees are preoccupied with renouncing Jesus as a 'sinner'. **They are Moses' disciples** setting themselves as judges of Jesus for his act in breaking the law by healing on the Sabbath, thus applying the Law as their guiding criterion. Indeed it should be remembered that for the rabbis the **Law (Torah) was a light** or lamp which gave illumination if properly understood (eg. Psalm 119v105). Yet it is the man previously blind who is shown as one who sees more clearly as he points out that God does not hear sinners and that Jesus has performed in curing him a healing not heard of since the world began. Again there seems the possibility that the evangelist is keen to suggest that **Light Jesus supersedes the Law** and hence cannot be condemned for giving the man his light on the Sabbath day.

A **battle scene** seems to ensue as the now 'son of light' seeks to enlighten the 'darkened' Pharisees. Relevant background to understanding John's intentions might be offered by the battle of light against darkness both in Zoroastrianism and in the **Dead Sea Scrolls**, though the connection of such background material with John is fiercely debated by scholars. The Pharisees, seen by Brown (pg380) to be malevolent, here fight back with abuse, perhaps indicative the argument is lost, and in consequence the man is cast out of the synagogue for the Pharisees conclude "Thou wast altogether born in sins, and dost thou teach us?"

At that point the man is found by Jesus and is called upon to believe that the very Jesus "that talketh with thee" is the son of man, a term which may be a veiled messianic title. Some have seen Jesus' identification as 'light' as being **messianic** as he fulfils, for example, Isaiah 9v2 'The people who walked in darkness have seen a great light'. The man commits himself, 'Lord I believe', which seems the response of a man truly brought through various stages of insight into appreciating Jesus' person. He has made a judgement about Christ and is enlightened by Light Jesus who has become the man's 'Lord' of light and salvation. **Jesus' position of importance** is brought out not only by the acknowledging term 'Lord' but also by the mention by the evangelist that the man 'worshipped' Jesus.

Jesus pronounces that his presence in the world is **"for judgement"**, for while there are those who have come to see from blindness there are those who now are made blind. He is now the judge and one might expect that the pharisees' interjection "Are we blind also?" would merely be answered in the affirmative. However, Jesus points out that blindness would excuse them for they would have no sin; it is because they claim to see that they are deservedly condemned for their sins truly remain. Jesus has taken no part in the debate itself but appears at the end of the passage to point out the issue of judgement.

Clearly the miracle together with the different dialogues is about light but in the sense that we have ourselves seen the **progress of a man to spiritual enlightenment and that man's witness as 'evidence'** to those unseeing and hence unbelieving. Those unbelievers are condemned for where there is the light of the world there is judgement for those who falsely claim to be enlightened, in this instance the Law light followed by the Pharisees has blinded and prevented them seeing what is the true light of the world and in consequence they are confirmed as being in the darkness. Thus in reality the passage has been a discourse on the **integration of light, witness and judgement** and not merely a glimpse of teaching on light.

With this in mind the **section Ch. 8v12-59** becomes meaningful in terms of Jesus as the light of the world. For to see v12, 'I am the light of the world', merely to introduce a section on witness (Barrett pg 333) is to misconstrue the evangelist's desire to appreciate that to be truly in the light one must 'see' the witness/es by which one is signposted to Jesus, and understand the judgemental consequences for not accepting the witness.

The passage in Ch. 8 as that in Ch. 9 is a discourse, but this time **the major speaker is Jesus himself**; he attempts to show the blindness of the Pharisees to his person and that their rejection of him engulfs them in blind sin, ironically that sin that they attribute to Jesus himself. As the discourse unfolds, with the repeated interjections of the Pharisees/Jews in open hostility, it is clear that the Pharisees are not to allow Jesus' statements to go unchallenged. The dualistic battle is enjoined as in Chapter 9 but this time the **antagonists are openly Jesus and the Pharisees**. However, it is possible that the controversial interchanges reflect the opposition from the Jews to Christianity at the time of the evangelist and represent his answers to the criticisms levelled at Jesus.

In v12 Jesus not only states 'I am the light of the world' but adds that his followers will not walk in the darkness but have that light of life. This statement sparks off the linguistic battle which seems to reflect a courtroom situation **again with Jesus on trial**. Thus the Jews accuse him of **bearing witness to himself** and this witness is therefore untrue as in keeping with their 'legal' understanding there need to be supporting witnesses. This is answered by Jesus as he suggests his witness and judgement are true as he has his **Father as his supporting witness**. He (or the later Johannine church) seems to detach himself from Judaism and 'your laws' (v17), and he further answers their interjection in v19 with an accusation that they do not know the Father hence they cannot know him.

It appears that one of the main purposes of the discourse is in fact to **establish Jesus' authority and his relationship with the Father**. So to know the Father enables a revelation of Jesus to be appreciated. Moreover, Jesus 'belongs' to the world above where the Father dwells, but has come 'forth from God' (v42) sent by the Father who seeks his glory (v50). In contrast his hearers are from the earthly world below. Thus they do not listen to the message that **Jesus is the messianic son of man** and conveys to them the words of his Father, though they will know that he is 'I am' when they have lifted up (normally interpreted as Jesus being put on the cross) the son of man (v28).

As the debate/trial continues, Jesus (or the evangelist) seeks to show them that he can offer them many things. He has God's words and can set them free from sin, show them the truth, and also ensure that those who listen to his words will not taste death. This last comment leads to the Jews commenting that Abraham has died as have the prophets, so who is Jesus claiming to be? **Is he greater than Abraham?**

This seems to be a leading question from the 'prosecution'. It seems similar to the question of the High Priest in the Synoptic's account of Jesus' trial, 'Are you the messiah?' Of course the Synoptic writers believe he is the messiah, Mark even has 'yes' (I am) answering in the affirmative. So too John appears to believe that **Jesus is truly greater than their patriarch**, though Jesus does not openly state he is in answer to their question. He merely repeats that the Father seeks his glory and that Abraham "rejoiced to see my day". Yet he is pressed, and asked "have you seen Abraham?" At this point and seemingly with pronouncing authority, Jesus states "truly, truly", the courtroom's 'this is the truth', and he avows **"before Abraham was, I am."**. The evangelist, as with his Logos theology in Chapter 1, is hinting at Jesus' pre-existence, here being 'before' Abraham, but also being above with the Father as 'I am'. So Jesus has both the seeming support of Abraham, who rejoiced to see Jesus' day, and his Father within his 'defence'. However, to the Jewish prosecutors these words are blasphemous and according to their law he must die, and "so they took up stones to throw at him" (v59); they become prosecutors, jury and judge all in an instance.

However, while Jesus the light of the world has to strangely 'hide himself' they do not have their way for he "went out of the temple". The impression given is of a turning away from their centre of Judaism leaving it confirmed in its darkness, ironic at the apparent festival of Tabernacles with its links with the temple candelabra.

The nature of the Jewish opposition should also be seen as an important and intended point of the evangelist. Naturally as opponents of Jesus they are not shown in a good light. As seen above they are unwilling to listen to his defence even with the 'big gun' witnesses he calls. Throughout the discourse **they misunderstand Jesus' words in typical Johannine fashion**. When in v20 Jesus comments on his going away they wonder "Will he kill himself?" rather than appreciating that he is to return to the Father. As he speaks further of the Father "They did not understand that he spoke to them of the Father" (v27); and when Jesus states (v52) that those keeping his words "will never taste death", they are now convinced he has a demon for even

Abraham has died. (Some have seen a possible link of the 'glory' (v50) and 'never tasting death' (v52) with Isaiah Ch. 60v1-2; if so then Jesus is the fulfilment of this enlightening glory.) Again they are judging on a 'literal' understanding of Jesus' words.

However, Jesus' **Jewish opponents are in reality being judged themselves**. They are in the spotlight with **Jesus as their prosecutor and judge** v26 "I have much to say about you and much to judge". They are clearly of an 'earthly' nature being from the world 'below' and destined to die in their sins. Yet it should be noted that in 8v30 the evangelist actually records that as Jesus spoke "**many believed in him**". It is to these that he subsequently speaks and nowhere are we told this audience changes up to the end of the chapter. Perhaps therefore surprisingly the 'believers' show what appears to be animosity. While a variety of suggestions have been made as to who these 'believers' are (see Carson 'The Gospel according to John', pg 346ff), as Carson himself notes the passage seems to show **those of 'fickle faith'** who really ought to show perseverence. They are told that to truly show their belief as disciples they must continue in Jesus' word, loyal to his teaching, then they will know the truth and be set free (v31-2).

These apparent Christian believers are clearly still in the darkness. Antagonistically they **claim** descent from Abraham and suggest **they do not need setting free** as they have never been in bondage; clearly this indicates their blindness to truth as throughout most of history the Jews seem to have been under the control of some power and they fail to appreciate they are being offered freedom from sin. Jesus points out in almost parabolic fashion (v34-6) that **they are enslaved by sin** but he is the son of the house with power to grant them freedom.

Jesus does not accept their empty claim to be Abraham's children for in wanting to kill him, they demonstrate **they are sons of the devil**. Likewise Jesus does not accept their further claim to be children of God; they are sons and followers of their murderous lying father the devil, who is the father of lies, which ironically prevents them seeing and believing the truth of Jesus' words. This is all the more tragic as in contrast Jesus gives life and truth. The words of the passage seem reminiscent of the teaching of John the Baptist in Mt. 3v9, Lk. 3v8. There may be a wider connection with the two Synoptic passages as

John the Baptist calls the people 'offspring of vipers' possibly to be translated as 'devils' children'.

They **resort to abuse** rather than argument in v48 "Are we not right in saying that you are a Samaritan and have a demon?" again reminiscent of the Synoptic Gospel's accusation that Jesus worked by the power of Beelzebul (eg. Mk. 3v22). For the evangelist this is ironical as they have themselves been accused of being children of the devil. Jesus naturally refutes their accusation pointing out his relationship with God who truly is his Father. In their final act of wanting to stone him they show they are murderous devil's children and Jesus leaves them to their own destiny of enslavement. It appears that if they were believing Christians at v30, at the end of the discourse they **have turned against Jesus** and seemingly have lost their light of the world. Perhaps, as Dodd has suggested, they were Judaising Christians those who were too over-zealous for the law. This would logically set them apart from those (Jesus or perhaps more understandably a church with a Johannine theology) who placed Jesus in, for them, the blasphemous 'I am' position.

The drama moves on into Ch. 9 where this destiny of **'judgement'** is to be pronounced upon them by Jesus for they fail to see even when an 'enlightening' sign is performed. The discourses of Ch. 8 and Ch. 9 demonstrate the **deliberate refusal of the Pharisees to be enlightened** by the 'light of the world', and his, his Father's, and the man born blind's witness. Such desire to remain outside the light is rejection and in turn signifies their own judgement by the light. While they judge others ironically the wheel comes round full circle upon themselves. They remain slaves of sin and unappreciative that someone whom they had judged because of his blindness to be 'born and bred in sin' actually comes to be set free and escape and hence to be a true child of Abraham because of Light Jesus.

▶Door of the Sheep discourse (Ch. 10v1-10)

The passage in which Jesus states 'I am the door of the sheep' is **pure monologue** apart from the evangelist's comment in v6. While separate comments will be made on the 'door' material it should be noted that it is closely linked with the picture of the shepherd caring for his sheep (to be enlarged upon from v11) and so the separation is a little artificial. For while for example 'door' and 'shepherd' are separated in v2, later Jesus becomes both (Barrett pg369).

Indeed there is actually **little material purely about Jesus as the door**. In vs1-3 Jesus indicates that while the shepherd enters the sheepfold through the door a thief or a robber climbs in another way. It is only to the shepherd that the doorkeeper opens the door (v4-5 are about the shepherd known and followed by his sheep in contrast to strangers from whom the sheep flee). The image of the door is reintroduced in v7 where Jesus actually uses the I am saying 'I am the door of the sheep'; in v9 he is the door through which a person enters to gain salvation and through which a person goes in and out to find pasture. There are those who are thieves and robbers whose plan is to steal, kill, and destroy. Yet Jesus is there to enable them to have 'abundant' life.

Reference to 'door' might be reminiscent to some Greeks as within **Greek literature** there is a door through which one enters heaven. Similarly **for Jews** there was a gate of heaven, seen by Jacob in his Bethel experience (Genesis 28v17) which could be opened by God (Psalm 78v23) or the 365 gates of heaven opened by angels (3 Baruch 6v13).

From this background, if there was a door/s in heaven then possibly it would also allow entrance into heaven; this may be the point the evangelist wishes to present—**Jesus as the heavenly door**. The picture thus created is that it is by passing through Door Jesus that **salvation and abundant life** are obtained. It is a simple picture yet one that may emphasise the need to act. One must actually enter the sheepfold by way of Jesus, who will aid by leading, to truly be saved. Some see a possible connection with the reference in Mt. Ch. 7v13-14 where one needs to enter by the narrow gate and to take the difficult way that leads to life.

However, the picture of Jesus as the door to heaven might contain **some problems**. It would seem that it could be **implied that the sheepfold is itself heaven**. While this might seem a sensible point, in v1 thieves and robbers can gain access to the sheepfold by climbing in another way and (v8 and v10) such characters are out to steal, kill, and destroy. It would seem questionable that these 'killers' will gain 'heaven' as their sheepfold as the evangelist does not seem to be implying that those will have salvation for they have avoided entering by the door which is that means of salvation. In what seems to some an echo of Numbers Ch. 27v15-17, it is also stated that sheep can go in and out of the sheepfold to gain pasturage so long as they pass through the door. It would seem a strange concept for those saved to go from heaven. Some have perhaps tried to avoid the difficulties by suggesting they came about through the fault of some redactor.

It has been suggested that the **sheepfold may be the 'church'**, thus indicating Door Jesus allows the church to be the place in which 'his' sheep gain salvation. The thieves and robbers might then be those who enter the church not to benefit the true Christians but to set themselves against them, not to give life but death. Beasley-Murray wonders if they might be leaders of some 'schism' group (pg169). Grayston suggests the possibility of chief priests and Pharisees (pg84), while perhaps more imaginatively Barrett (pg369) offers the suggestion that they refer "not to a person but a class. Messianic pretenders may be in mind; perhaps more probably the many 'saviours' of the Hellenistic world."

Perhaps caution must be exercised not to drift towards automatically interpreting the passage in allegorical terms but to **concentrate on the essential Christological focus of Jesus as the means 'through' which salvation is gained**. It then may be as Barrett suggests (pg367) neither parable nor allegory but "symbolic discourse in which symbolism and straightforward statement alternate and stand side by side."

Also rather than remembering past experiences associated with the 'door', as for example God raining 'physical' manna through the doors of heaven (Psalm 78v4), it should be appreciated that it is now Jesus who rains upon the people **abundant life of an eternal nature**.

It should also be noted that in v7 Jesus is the 'door of the sheep' whereas in v1 he was the door of the 'fold' of the sheep. It may be that the evangelist means no difference for Jesus is still the means into salvation. Yet possibly the concentration in v7 is now on the sheep, and a **more personal intention may be in mind**. Here John is thinking of the 'what/for whom' rather than merely of an actual place, the 'where'. He may want to establish the salvation that is to be enjoyed by the sheep not to indicate where that salvation is to be enjoyed.

▶ Good Shepherd discourse (Ch. 10v1-18)

Mention has been made above re. v2,3,4 of the figure of a shepherd as given entrance into the sheepfold by the doorkeeper, and leading his sheep who follow him because they know his voice. The shepherd is contrasted with those strangers (v5) from whom the sheep flee.

From v11 the evangelist expands on those introductory observations in what Grayston describes (pg xviii) as the most striking example of an **instructive monologue** which (Bultmann pg363) states is the last to people in general, perhaps as Jesus' final appeal to the world.

In v11 Jesus makes the 'I am' claim to be 'the good shepherd'. Schnackenburg (pg295) points out that "In the Orient of ancient times, as well as in Greece and the Hellenistic world, the use of 'shepherd' as a **designation for a divine or human ruler was widespread**". Thus **non-Jewish gods** like Marduk featured as shepherds, as too did **Babylonian kings** and **Greek heroes**. Bultmann (pg367) suggests that the image of shepherd is most clear in Mandaen literature. The scholar sees a direct link between the **Gnostic revealer-shepherd** and Jesus as shepherd in the Fourth Gospel.

However, many scholars are unconvinced by Bultmann's suggestions; Schnackenburg (pg295) argues that Jesus is different from the Gnostic revealer-shepherd as with reference to the latter there is nowhere a mention of life-sacrifice as there is in John's Gospel. Also Schnackenburg argues that Jesus as shepherd bears no ruler-like features and so he questions links between a non-Jewish background and the Fourth Gospel. Similarly, while there is (Carson, pg382) "extensive use of sheep/shepherd imagery in the **Synoptic Gospels** (e.g. Mt. 9v36; 18v12-14; Mk. 6v34; 14v27; Lk. 15v1-7)", Carson still observes that it is a dubious enterprise to detect direct dependence on one or more Synoptic account.

Some suggest a possible link with John's picture of Jesus and **Philo** who sees both God and His first-born son or 'word' as shepherd, while others favour a link with the Old Testament. There are many references in the **Old Testament** to God being 'shepherd'; for example in Psalm 23v1, 'The Lord is my shepherd', Psalm 77v20 'Thou didst lead thy people like a flock', and Isaiah 40 v11 'He will feed his flock like a shepherd'. Certainly in John's Gospel Good Shepherd Jesus cares for and leads his sheep even being willing to give up his life for them. While the 'Good Shepherd' is to be seen as a title not a mere comparison (or contrast) with shepherds (Bultmann pg364), nevertheless 'goodness' is truly exemplified by that dying for the sheep.

Moreover, surely contrast is used by the evangelist to emphasise the **total difference in the actions and motives of Good Shepherd Jesus** with those who are merely hired to look after the sheep. The contrast for Marsh (pg400) is to be seen in the character and quality of the role. In v12 the evangelist indicates that the sheep have no relationship with the hireling—there is no binding belonging. Thus, when danger comes, for example from the wolf, they care for their own safety, not that of the sheep and so they run away leaving the sheep to be caught and scattered by their foe.

There seems a strong case for suggesting a link with this Johannine discourse and **Ezekiel Chapter 34** where the selfish shepherd rulers have been looking after themselves (v2-3) and have ruled so uncaringly and selfishly that they have scattered the sheep who have become food for the wild beasts (v5). Elsewhere in the Old Testament God, not surprisingly, is angry with such shepherd leaders (Zech Ch. 10), and pronounces 'woe' upon them (Jer. 23v1).

Again, Good Shepherd Jesus in contrast does not run away when danger comes, but because (v 14) he has such an intimate 'knowledge' of them and for his sheep (as he also has with the Father) **he lays down his life**. For Bultmann (pg367) such a reciprocal relationship is not to be found in Old Testament material, and neither, according to Barrett (pg374/5), is the dying of the shepherd, rather it is "based specifically upon the crucifixion as a known historical fact." For Beasley-Murray (pg170) the language of metaphor has become a Kerygmatic affirmation, that is the 'proclaimed' (preached) message of the Early Church.

One should perhaps again beware of allegorising the passage, yet there may be in the evangelist's mind a desire to emphasise the 'goodness' of Good Shepherd Jesus partly to indicate how far short of that goodness are the 'hirelings'. These clearly are **bad shepherds**, purely selfish. In view of the earlier mentioned background material it is not surprising that these hirelings are generally equated with the bad rulers of the Jews at the time of Jesus (or/and at the time of the evangelist). The problem, if thinking allegorically, then arises as to whom does the 'wolf' refer? Perhaps it may be linked to those earlier mentioned 'thieves and robbers' and be interpreted as previously suggested. Or perhaps it is merely introduced as an effective part of the story's description, portraying what might be a situation 'sufficiently familiar to him' (Barrett pg375).

When one focuses further on the good shepherd his goodness is demonstrated by his **concern 'solely for the good of the sheep'** (Marsh pg396), and so he is willing to put his life 'on the line' (Grayston pg84), shrinking from no sacrifice (Sanders and Mastin pg250). God loves Jesus (v17) "because **I lay down my life**". He epitomises 'self-giving', dying 'vicariously', for the good shepherd focuses only on his sheep; in giving his life for others he actually gives life to others. Yet for John he gives his life because of his goodness rather than having it taken away because of badness for (v18) "No one takes it from me, but I lay it down of my own accord". However, Barrett suggests (pg 377) this **'voluntary' act of the heroic shepherd** is an 'important part of **Christian apologetic'**, as it would be an argument against the possible accusation from opponents that Jesus must merely have been a guilty and executed criminal. Also **authority of Jesus** would be portrayed by his statement (v18) "I have power to lay it down, and I have power to take it again". Jesus is not merely the suffering Good Shepherd, he is also to John the rising glorious Lord.

In v16 Jesus alludes to other sheep 'not of this fold' which also must be brought in. They will hear his voice and there will then be 'one flock, one shepherd'. Those **sheep 'not of this fold' have generally been identified with Gentiles** so indicating the universal interest of Jesus and/or the evangelist. There seems a clear **desire to indicate unity** of the sheep under their unifying shepherd. It may be that at the time of writing the evangelist was aware of some division, from those wolves harrying the flock or from the robbers and thieves whoever they may represent. The call is then to unite with the 'introduction' of Jesus' words indicating his desire for that to be so, though Grayston (pg84) interestingly suggests opposition against Jesus comes because almost ironically he is seen as 'sheep stealing' Jews from their Mosaic allegiance. It is also possible that the evangelist wishes to make a further link with Ezekiel Chapter 34 where the evil shepherds/rulers, acting against the interest of the sheep, will not foil God's intentions as he will raise up the **messianic descendant of**

David as their 'one shepherd' (v23) who will 'feed them and be their shepherd'. There is also in Ps. Sol 17 the picture of the messianic king acting as faithful and righteous shepherd. For John, Jesus is this messianic shepherd.

Additional material (v19-39)—As a result of Jesus' words there is a division of opinion about him; some see him as possessed by the devil while others appreciate that such words are not demon inspired and his power to open the eyes of a blind man is not that of a demon. In v22 the evangelist indicates it was the time of the Jewish **Feast of Dedication** and that Jesus at the time was walking in the temple, in particular in the portico of Solomon. This may be a simple descriptive detail yet if symbolic it may be adding the 'comment' that Jesus' words far from being demon based, are, as those of Solomon before him, words of wisdom. Also the setting of the Feast of Dedication, when Jews celebrated the re-purification of the temple following its desecration by Antiochus Epiphanes (168-165 BCE), might hint at the presence of something which was tainting the temple again and which needed the act of Jesus in dying to sacrificially make it clean. Beasley-Murray (pg177) suggests that the reference to Dedication is highly significant as the **meaning of the Feast 'finds its ultimate fulfilment in the mission of Jesus'.**

The **shepherd messiah Jesus** has arrived in God's temple and the Jews at least seem to appreciate that as a possibility for they ask Jesus to tell them plainly if he is the messiah (v24). He responds that he has already told them but they are unbelievers even though his works bear witness to him. They are told their lack of belief is because they are not Jesus' sheep. For his sheep there is to be a 'knowing' relationship within the gift of eternal life, and the protection that the 'Father' provides for them.

Jesus' own intimate relationship with the Father is again stressed by the evangelist with 'I and the Father are one' (v30), for while they are both shepherds they are also in reality 'one'. For Barrett (pg382) this is a oneness of love and obedience as well as a oneness of 'essence', literally 'one thing' (Sanders and Mastin pg258). However, on this point, Beasley-Murray argues the evangelist intends only to suggest they are one in action 'not in person' (pg174) and that the conclusions of Jesus' divinity drawn from the statement by the early church fathers was not in the mind of the evangelist. In answer to Beasley-Murray, it often appears in John's Gospel that opponents of Jesus seem to 'appreciate' what is the opposite of the truth. Here in accusing him of blaspheming they may then merely demonstrate he truly shares this actual oneness with the Father.

However, the disbelieving Jews do only see Jesus' words as blasphemous and (v31) want to arrest him (v39) and stone him (echoing their desire in chapter 8). Clearly from the words of Jesus within v32-38 it appears that their opposition to him goes against the evidence of his good works; also in Psalm 82v6, cited in v34, the people are called 'gods' and sons of God so how can his words be blasphemy? In v36 Jesus is presented as the one consecrated and sent into the world by the Father and it may be implied he has thus made a claim to be **Son of God**. Further his works also demonstrate **the Father is in him and he is in the Father**, but the Jews are not persuaded by argument and again try to arrest him. However, while no details are given by the evangelist, Jesus escaped from their hands (v39), for at this point the 'shepherd' is not to be robbed of his life, for when his hour comes he will 'lay it down' of his own accord.

Later (Ch. 21v15-17) when the disciples' pastoral leader Jesus is to leave them he instructs Peter to take on the role of feeding his lambs and tending and feeding his sheep. Jesus' concern for the flock never wavers or diminishes and the church is to be encouraged to follow that example.

▶Resurrection and Life discourse (Ch. 11v1-46)

Dodd argues (pg363) that the Lazarus 'pericope' contains a **large proportion of discourse in the form of a dialogue** in which there are **numerous interlocutors** and that the pericope in pattern is different from the normal pattern of sign then discourse. For as both Dodd (pg363) and Barrett (pg20) suggest, in Ch. 11 **narrative and dialogue are woven together**, and Beasley-Murray (pg184) notes that narrative is interspersed with dialogue.

However, while this discourse may be a unified narrative/dialogue presentation, the following comments will concentrate on the dialogue (discourse) aspects.

John sets the scene for the event by Martha and Mary indicating that their brother Lazarus, whom Jesus loved, is ill. Jesus' statement (v4), presumably accepted by the evangelist as one reason for the 'sign', emphasises that Lazarus' illness is not unto death but for the **glory both of God and the Son of God**.

However, to show this 'glory' the evangelist also needs to **indicate aspects of death**. So when, after staying 'two days longer in the place where he was', Jesus makes a simple statement indicating he is to return again into Judea, words of warning are given by the disciples for they question Jesus' intention as the 'Jews were but now **seeking to stone you**'. Moreover, **Lazarus does indeed 'die'**, and when the disciples actually appreciate that point, Thomas tells the others that they should accompany Jesus **that they may die with him**, foreshadowing not only Jesus' death but also possibly what was within the evangelist's own sitz im leben, the later fate of Christians. Martha's later reluctance to follow Jesus' instruction to take away the stone is because she is afraid that her dead brother's body will be **decomposing and giving off an odour**.

In the earlier healing of the Officer's son the evangelist painted a picture of the son being 'ill', 'at the point of death' and his father asking Jesus to 'come down before my child dies'. Yet this focus was replaced by emphasis on life; Jesus tells him 'your son will live' and the servants confirm this which convinces him that Jesus' words 'Your son will live' had effected the cure. So too in the Lazarus incident **'death' becomes overshadowed by aspects of 'life'**; initially Jesus had affirmed that Lazarus' illness would not end in death, and for the evangelist this is to be achieved because Jesus is the life-giver.

The evangelist is keen to **show the nature of Jesus' person** for there is a need to appreciate who Jesus is and what can be achieved by him. From the outset it is clear that Jesus can and will 'awaken' Lazarus. Yet in order to truly and fully demonstrate Jesus' life-giving capacity Lazarus does physically need to die (perhaps this is the reason for Jesus staying 'two days longer in the place where he was') then in reality Jesus will be the 'resurrection and the life'.

When Martha meets Jesus she shows some appreciation of his power stating that **Lazarus would have been saved from death if Jesus had been there**, and that God will give Jesus whatever he asks. Yet when Jesus pronounces that her brother is to rise, Martha voices what appears to reflect the Pharisaic belief in 'a final resurrection on the last day to life of the age to come or to judgement' (Barrett pg395) and so demonstrates that her 'I know' is mere expectation. In typical Johannine fashion she **'misunderstands'** what Jesus is indicating to her.

So Jesus issues the 'I am' statement, **'I am the resurrection and the life'**. Not only is Jesus again asserting that life comes to people because he is 'I am' but that in this instance this is to be demonstrated even in terms of giving life to someone who was dead. Perhaps Jesus is the 'living Redeemer' of Job Ch. 19v25ff who will stand on the earth so that for a person "after my skin has been destroyed then my flesh will see God". Some may also see a connection of Jesus' action and person with the reference in Sotah 9v15 to the Lord being the quickener of the dead. Because Jesus is present so too is the resurrection; **the expected end age has arrived**. For the evangelist this 'quickening' is not to be in the last days, nor as in Wisdom literature a gift to the righteous through Wisdom, for Martha is to see her brother given back life 'now' by him who is resurrection and life itself.

Martha (v21) and Mary (v32) showed that they were aware that if Jesus had been there then their brother would not have died. Also the crowd's question (v37) 'Could not he who opened the eyes of the blind man have kept this man from dying?' seems to imply some appreciation of the **power of Jesus**, but there almost seems an accusation of callousness on the part of Jesus for not saving Lazarus. Yet for the evangelist **Jesus was definitely not unfeeling**; he loved Lazarus and his sisters and journeyed to them; when he saw Mary and the Jews crying he was 'deeply moved in spirit and troubled' and also wept. Christians would believe Jesus did indeed historically/physically have power to stop death, but as stated earlier Lazarus had to die for Jesus to be truly shown to be 'the resurrection and the life', for the sisters and the crowd are to witness something they may have thought unbelievable. The evangelist wishes to capture the truth of Jesus' earlier words that they are to witness something "for the glory of God, so that the Son of God may be glorified" (v4).

From the opening verses, the sign leads up to the **moment when this glory would be demonstrated**. The length of time Lazarus has been in the tomb adds emphasis to the spectacular nature of Jesus' action; apart from the suggested decomposition of the body, the

Jews believed that after four days even Lazarus' spirit would have departed from his body. Also a **contrast** can surely be made between this raising from the dead and its **other New Testament counterparts**; for Jairus' Daughter (Mk. Ch.5), Dorcas (raised by Peter—Acts Ch.9) and Eutychus (raised by Paul—Acts Ch. 20) had only 'recently' died, and the widow's son (Lk. Ch. 7) is only on the way to be buried. Similarly in the **Old Testament**, Elijah is given the Widow of Zarephath's son soon after death (1 Kings Ch. 17v17ff), and while Elisha has to journey to the Shunammite woman's son it appears to be the same day as he has died when Elisha arrives (2 Kings Ch. 4v18ff).

When Lazarus is called from the tomb by Jesus the barriers of death are gloriously overthrown, and the conquering Resurrection and Life Jesus truly makes the eternal life relationship with the Father a reality. It also **foreshadows** what is to be an even more **glorious resurrection of Jesus himself** which enables all believers to be gathered 'into one' (v52). Jesus truly is the resurrection and the life; this is demonstrated through the physical raising of Lazarus, for now as stated would happen (Ch. 5v28) those in the tombs hearing Jesus' voice have indeed come forth to the resurrection of life. For the evangelist the present reality of eschatological salvation is not only here but to be freely distributed when Jesus, soon after this incident, dies and comes forth from the tomb. For those who might see a connection with the rising of **Tammuz**, a god of Mesopotamian religion rising as he does in the spring, it should be noted that Jesus does not die in the autumn to rise in the spring but just rises after two days. Moreover, Jesus' action is not linked with fertility but with establishing the eternal life relationship with his Father. Jesus' death, like that of Lazarus, may have been itself preventable but Jesus had to die to demonstrate, as he had indicated in chapter 10, his love as shepherd for his believing 'friends' which he would show in dying for them.

Perhaps a more sustainable link with Jesus' death and resurrection would be with the **saviour of the mystery religions** sent to die and rise to win human beings immortality and union with God. Bultmann argued strongly for a connection with the Mandaean soteriological myth where the son of the king of light is sent to earth to aid humans to their true home in heaven. The son himself returns to heaven to gather into heaven the 'sparks of light' of believers when they die.

However, even if it is admitted there may seem links it cannot be concluded that the evangelist is dependent on such material.

This aspect of 'believing' seems to be another feature of the Lazarus discourse. Jesus' statement in v11 that he is to go to awaken Lazarus, the friend of them all, who 'has fallen asleep' is in typical fashion taken literally by the disciples, who seem unable to discern his analogical hints. They say that Lazarus will recover from sleep, though the 'recover' may unwittingly be an indication of how Lazarus will indeed recover from what was more than mere sleep. Jesus then tells them 'openly' that Lazarus is dead and adds that he is glad for their sake that he was not there for he will go on to perform the sign 'so that you (the disciples) may believe'

Martha too is told that a believer who dies will live and a living believer will not die.

Jesus asks her "Do you believe this?". The man previously blind (Ch. 9) was asked 'Do you believe…?' and now it is Martha's turn. Like the blind man she expresses her belief, but rather than to Jesus being Son of man, **she states he is 'the Christ, the Son of God'** the arrival of whom the Jews awaited (v26). Martha has answered in an almost creedal fashion. This is the way the evangelist wishes all to answer; for what Martha states seems to be the apparent requirement, expressed in Ch. 20v31, of that believer who is to gain eternal life.

Believing seems foremost in the mind of Jesus, and it might be supposed of the evangelist, when Jesus prays to the Father (v41-2); for in his prayer Jesus expresses that he knows himself that God always hears him and has merely spoken 'on account of the people standing by, that they may believe that thou didst send me.' Indeed many as a result of the resurrection sign he performs 'believed in him' (v45).

However, characteristically John presents **the antithesis of believing**, for eventhough they had witnessed the miracle, some went and reported Jesus to the Pharisees. They had witnessed the miracle but failed to appreciate it as a 'sign'. Some have wondered if there is a link with the Johannine passage and the **parable of the rich man and Lazarus in Lk Ch 16v16ff**. Indeed some have argued that the Johannine passage may be the evangelist's 'production' based on the Lucan parable. Certainly it should be noted that there is no mention in the Synoptic Gospels of a Lazarus who was the brother of Martha and Mary. Also in the parable the Lazarus there dies, and v31, where Abraham in the parable makes the comment that "neither will they be convinced if someone should rise from the dead", seems close to the Johannine point about disbelief. However, in contrast to the Johannine material, Lazarus in the Lucan parable is not raised from the dead.

It should be noted that the Pharisees were a Jewish group who believed in the resurrection yet they are shown to oppose Resurrection and Life Jesus. Ironically they join forces (11v47) with chief priests who in contrast, being Sadducees, refused to believe in the resurrection. They call together a meeting of the central Jewish Council, the Sanhedrin, showing their fear that because Jesus "performs many signs. If we let him go on thus, everyone will believe in him" (v48).

Indeed, this and the other 'many signs' which Jesus performed led to the **decision of the Council to execute Jesus**, though with ironic poignancy Caiaphas, the High Priest, states that one man should die for the people so that the whole nation should not perish for Jesus' sacrifice will truly enable the world to have the opportunity of 'life'. Yet also ironically those rejecting Resurrection and Life Jesus, in keeping with the text of Sanhedrin 10v1 as they "say there is no resurrection of the dead" they "will have no share in the world to come".

At the beginning of the discourse (v9) Jesus indicated that no one can stumble in the hours of daylight as that person 'sees the light of this world'. As Jesus had identified himself in earlier chapters as the light of the world the statement appears to indicate the need to walk in the light of Christ. One will stumble without that light being 'in him' indicating that the light is to be an inner guide from Christ who will be within. The Pharisees and the other non-believers chose the destiny of 'stumbling about' blind to the truth that Jesus could even give life eternal to the dead. Instead at the end of the discourse they fulfil what had been indicated at its beginning in determining, and eventually carrying out, the execution of Jesus. However, even in this they failed, for how could they extinguish the life from him who was the giver of eternal life?

▶Way, truth and life discourse (Ch. 14v1-14)

In this discourse, which is part of the larger complex referred to as the 'farewell discourses', Jesus is **preparing his disciples for his departure in death and his return to the Father**. Beasley-Murray (pg263) notes that this discourse is unlike those previously considered as it is addressed to Jesus' disciples and is thus 'fundamentally the testament of Jesus to the church' and also (pg222) that the farewell discourses in general may have been fashioned by combining sayings from various sources.

This message in the discourse is presented with limited interlocution from Thomas (v5) and Philip (v8).

One of the main features of the discourse is **Jesus' 'going away'**. Previously in Ch. 13v33ff Jesus has spoken about his going and that at present his disciples could not come with him. Peter had enquired where Jesus was going, and when told he could not go with Jesus at that time but would later, Peter impetuously had questioned why he could not go with Jesus as he was willing to die for him. This in turn had led to Jesus predicting Peter's denial of him. Thus the 'going' is reintroduced in Chapter 14. In fact Grayston (pg104) considers 13v31-14v31 to be a self-contained unit.

Yet in chapter 14 the message of Jesus is one of **consolation and reassurance**. Even though he is 'going away' the disciples should not be troubled in heart but 'believe in God, believe also in me'. Grayston (pg115) suggests the Greek for this verse means that the disciples are not to let their 'resolution be upset (or intimidated); thus, Jesus is reinforcing their courage rather than confirming their anxiety by telling them not to fear. He is to go away in order that he can prepare a place for them in the habitations of the Father and that they can be re-united with him there. In v3 his reference to 'I will **come again**' (also later in v18 'I will not leave you comfortless; I will come to you') may be a reference to the Parousia; if it is it would be a rare indication of Jesus' second coming for most scholars argue that John has reinterpreted the Parousia in the coming of the Paraclete.

Jesus indicates that the disciples know the way where he is going, but Thomas interjects that as they don't know where he is going how can they know the way. He seems to want to know the way just as the Psalmists had appealed to God 'Make me know thy ways O Lord' (Ps. 25v4) or 'Teach me thy way O Lord' (Ps. 27v11; Ps. 86v11). Thomas' interlocution seems merely to act as a means of extending the discourse with clarifying words from Jesus.

In v6 Jesus makes the '**I am the way**' statement. Immediately it is pointed out that 'no one comes to the Father, but by me'. This seems to indicate that **Way Jesus is that which one travels to approach the Father**, though there is no apparent connection with Mt Ch. 7v14 where the way to life is along a hard 'way'. In John's Gospel there seems a hint of Christian exclusivism in that there is no other way to the Father but by Jesus. The early church even called Christianity 'The Way' (**Acts** Ch. 9v2; 19v9) and voiced these opinions, for example in **Hebrews** Ch. 10v19 where Jesus opened the new and living way through the curtain to God, and in **Ephesians** Ch. 2v18 where people are shown to have access to God through Jesus and his spirit. As Barrett states (pg458) '**there is no access to God independent of him** (Jesus)'. Jesus may be stating he is himself the fullest revelation of God available to man (Sanders & Mastin pg323). In v7 it is shown that knowledge of the Father, presumably in terms of the fellowship of a knowing relationship, is made available by knowing Way Jesus. Jesus further adds 'Henceforth you know him (the Father) and have seen him' which may indicate that the revelation of the Father is now witnessed by Jesus' followers fulfilling the indication in Ch. 1v18 that the only Son makes the Father known.

Yet the discourse then seems to move away from consideration of Jesus as the Way and further enlarges on the introduced **relationship of Jesus with the Father**. In what may be an examination by the evangelist of the mutuality of the Father and Son, Jesus, in response to Philip's interjection, another characteristic **misunderstanding**, (v8) 'Lord show us the Father, and we shall be satisfied', is able to make his meaning plain and draw out this relationship of 'integration'.

The 'I am' statement in v6 apart from indicating Way Jesus also adds '(I am...) **the truth**'. In this section there may seem to be no discussion of 'truth' but in reality Way Jesus is the revelation of God 'in truth', and for Beasley-Murray (pg252) Jesus is the way because he is truth. Schnackenburg (pg228) writes that the "Son embodies in himself the divine truth which means life for believers and so becomes the 'way' for all who seek salvation". As in the Moffatt translation of v6 Jesus is 'the true (and living) way', indeed **Jesus is the 'true' 'way' to 'life'** for 'life' is also indicated within the 'I am' saying. This may not be realised by the uncomprehending Philip but for believers there is the opportunity to appreciate that to see Truth Jesus is to 'truly' be in the Father's presence; perhaps again there is a hint of Christian exclusivism and its **replacement of Torah-based Judaism** for as Grayston notes (pg78) in the Qumran writings the Torah was regarded as truth. There is then no need to say 'Show us the Father' for that seems to indicate not only a misunderstanding but a lack of belief that Jesus is in the Father and the Father is in Jesus. Nor is there a need for Jesus to teach this truth for to manifest himself is to manifest God in truth.

Again some have seen a connection of Truth Jesus with **Old Testament** references. In Psalm 31v5 the psalmist believes he has been redeemed by 'God of truth' which the Johannine community may come to see is what Jesus accomplishes. It seems a strong case can be made for John being influenced by the Psalms in his presentation of Jesus. In both Psalm 25 and 86, cited above for reference to the 'way', the psalmists also speak of 'truth' (in Psalm 25v10 'the ways of the Lord are mercy and truth' and Psalm 86v11 'Teach me thy way O Lord that I may walk in thy truth'). Also in Psalm 86 God is stated to abound in 'truth'. So too in John's Gospel 'way', 'truth' and God (as 'I am') are connected in Jesus.

Thus Jesus (v10ff) states he speaks not on his own authority implying he has the authoritative backing of the Father, and that the Father dwelt in Jesus performing his works. Yet the disciples are **asked if they believe** this; there is a need and a call for them to believe the statement of Jesus or to believe in him because of the works which are performed. This **apparent emphasis on believing** is continued with the addition that such belief will enable those believers to do works Jesus himself performs, or even greater works, enabled by Jesus' return to the Father. The believer will receive whatever he asks in Jesus' name for the glorification of the Father in the Son. The 'truly, truly' (double 'amen') itself emphasises that Jesus' 'true' words will be accomplished. This is in keeping with the Hebrew truth **'emeth'** which Barclay (pg279) points out is truth 'in the sense of fidelity, reliability, trustworthiness, faithfulness. It is the truth in the sense in which a lover will say, 'I will be true to you.' Barrett further indicates (pg280) that the Greek word **'aletheia'** means 'truth as distinguished from falsehood, and .... that which is real and genuine as opposed to that which is unreal and counterfeit'. In the Manual of Discipline of the

Dead Sea Scrolls truth (light) is that which directs the way of man and which opposes perversity (darkness). Eventually truth will be victorious and man will be made clean by God's Spirit of truth.

It should be added that for John 'Truth' Jesus is the opposite of what the devil ruler of the world is. **The devil has 'nothing to do with truth** because there is no truth in him', he is a liar speaking 'according to his own nature' (8v44) yet ironically Jesus, because he speaks the truth, is not believed, rather they want to kill him. (See also earlier comments on Ch. 8). The 'darkened' world servants of their father the devil fail to see Jesus is the absolute (Platonic?) truth/reality. Later in chapter 14 (v30) Jesus speaks of the prince of the world coming and this is none other than Satan, though he has no power over Jesus. It is true that Jesus is going to be killed but this is not as a result of the devil's work rather it is Jesus doing what the Father wishes and has commanded him to do. Jesus' 'going' is thus merely a movement willingly forward to the cross.

▶**Additional material** (v15-31)—A new direction in the discourse is introduced in Ch. 14v15-17 with the first of the **Paraclete** sayings (see 'Holy Spirit' booklet for full treatment). In connection with Jesus as 'I am...the truth' the Paraclete is identified as the **'Spirit of truth'** who will dwell in them though the world will not receive the Paraclete. The Paraclete will also (v26) be sent by the Father in Jesus' name in order to teach them and remind them of Jesus' words. Also it should be noted that in v19 'because I live, you will live also'; they will be enthused with that living quality that is 'truly' bestowed by him who is 'I am....the life'.

The Way to Truth in the Old Testament and the writings of the Qumran community is through **performing the commands of God**, acting according to his discipline; this may have led to Torah being identified with Truth. In Deuteronomy Ch. 5v32-33 men must walk in the way which the Lord their God had commanded them, while in Proverbs Ch. 6v23 the reproofs of discipline are the way to life and the commandment is a lamp and the teaching a light.

This background material may be what causes the evangelist to record in 14v15 that Jesus states that **if they love him they will keep his commandments**, which is re-echoed in v21 where Jesus adds that such loving will in turn be returned both by the Father and Jesus and Jesus will manifest himself to the 'lover'. For Grayston (pg119) love is more than affection and devotion, it is keeping instructions and heeding what Jesus says, though really he only says one thing, his new commandment, that they should love one another. He will demonstrate this love himself on the cross.

Judas, not Iscariot, acts as an interlocutor in v22 voicing perhaps an intriguing question for later Christians, namely why should Jesus manifest himself to his disciple followers rather than the world. Alas the intriguing question seems side-stepped for Jesus makes further comments about the Father and himself making their home with the one who loves Christ. This theme of 'loving' is later amplified in the True Vine discourse (15 v9ff).

Chapter 14 ends (v27ff) with Jesus making comments that take us back to the opening verses of the chapter which some scholars have noted is characteristic of John's Gospel and which linguistically is referred to as 'inclusion'. The disciples are not to let their hearts be troubled nor should they be afraid, the reason being that they are to be left with the gift of Jesus' **'peace'**. Jesus contrasts his peace with that of the world although no details of that contrast are given; the reader can only surmise. Yet it may be intended that Jesus' peace is to be seen as an 'inner' dimension affecting their 'hearts'. If they truly loved him they ought not to be miserable but as Jesus states (v28) they should rather rejoice that he is **going away to the Father who 'is greater than I'**. This statement naturally raises questions about the status of Jesus and his relationship, his mutuality and oneness with the Father. There appears a dichotomy in John's Gospel as Jesus often seems to be given the status of divinity yet at the same time he seems 'inferior' to the Father. It is possible that Jesus (or the evangelist) is reflecting that in his 'above' state the Father is greater than Jesus in his earthly state, though when Jesus returns to his prior Logos abode then such a differentiation will disappear.

▶The true vine discourse (Ch. 15v1-17)

In Ch. 15v1-17 Jesus presents a discourse on himself as the 'true vine' again introduced with the 'I am' words. The verses (and those following to Ch. 16v17) are what may be termed **'pure monologue'**, Jesus alone speaking to his disciples **without interruption**.

Verses 1-6, which have been acknowledged as having an apparent

allegorical character (eg Sanders and Mastin, pg336), open with Jesus identifying himself as the 'true vine'. The word **'true'**, debated in part within the previous material, has similarly been linked with the philosophy of **Plato**. It is often taken as meaning 'real' and thus portrays Jesus as that which truly is the 'real' vine. For Plato that would mean Jesus is not a shadow or mere likeness of what a vine may be, he is the vine in all its absolute sense. Jesus is no copy he is the genuine article. Moreover his absolute vine nature links him with the divine; for Jesus is not like 'a' vine he is 'the' 'true' vine (Bultmann, pg4).

While this Platonic philosophy may not have directly influenced John, it is clear that the evangelist wishes to **differentiate between Jesus** who is in absolute ('I am') reality the Vine **and any other 'vine'** that his audience might recall. For example he may be hinting that the **golden vine** depicted in Herod's temple is but a symbol while Jesus is the Vine itself. Yet most commentators suggest Jewish **Old Testament** background material regarding the vine Israel is in the mind of Jesus or the evangelist; possibly there is a desire to suggest that 'True' Vine Jesus is even **superior to Wisdom** symbolised by the vine in Ecclesiasticus.

However frequently **Israel is identified as the vine**, but rather than as 'true', particularly in its sense of 'faithfulness', vine Israel **produces only 'wild grapes'** (Isaiah Ch. 5v2; Jeremiah Ch. 2v21) even though it was sown with the choicest vines of pure seed. This is also the picture in such New Testament passages as Mt. Ch. 21v33ff where the wicked vinedressers refuse to give the fruit that is required while in the Old Testament the luxuriant vine Israel has a false heart (Hosea Ch. 10v2).

So for the evangelist 'True Vine' Jesus would be the way to describe him who is the **opposite to such a degenerate people**. The **'true' differentiates Jesus from the Judaism** of the past with its 'false' growth and lack of 'emeth' (faithfulness). In contrast Jesus is concerned that his branches produce 'fruit' and even 'more fruit' (v2), possibly simply stressing the need to live the life of a Christian disciple (Barrett pg474). As in Isaiah Ch. 5v2 **God the Father is there as the vinedresser** doing all that is possible to enable the branches to produce such fruit. He even takes away the fruitless branches for fruitfulness is a requirement rather than a desired possibility.

The branches are identified by Jesus as 'of mine' and thus are none other than his followers, his disciples, and no doubt for the evangelist the members of the Christian community. There is clearly the opportunity for growth yet there is an apparent warning that even disciples can be taken away if unfruitful. Thus, for the follower of Jesus there is, as Bultmann comments (pg535), **promise and yet threat**. For just as for John eschatological **salvation** is available to the believer so too is **judgement** if they fail to 'abide' in Vine Jesus. One might be reminded of how Judas Iscariot had seemingly been washed by Jesus (Ch. 13) yet he went on to betray Vine Jesus. For even though the believers may have been 'made clean' by Jesus' words, **they still must 'abide'**.

This **mutual indwelling** (Barrett, pg474) is the message of vs 4-6. The disciples are called to abide in Jesus for he too abides in them. Moreover such indwelling is what is necessary in order to bring about the production of the required fruit. There is no other way; they must be united with the vine for 'without me you can do nothing' (v5). The **faithless Israel of the past** had only been fit to be devoured (Isaiah Ch. 5v5), burned (Ezek Ch. 15v1-8), and consumed by fire (Ezek Ch. 19v10ff). So in John's Gospel, failure to remain united will bring about destruction; just like the branch separated from the life-giving sap of the vine will wither away and will be 'gathered, thrown into the fire and burned' (v6). Barrett suggests (pg470) that the evangelist in his discourse has transformed Isaiah Ch. 5v1-7 from eschatological crisis to the life of the church; instead of about Israel it becomes a Christological definition.

Yet the passage from v7 does not concentrate (as the Old Testament seems to) on admonition and judgement but on the **results and rewards for abiding in the vine**. Abiding in Christ and allowing his words (of cleansing) to abide in them means all their requests will be granted. They will bear much fruit and so demonstrate their true discipleship by which they will ensure God is glorified.

It may be suggested that if Isaiah Ch. 5 was in the evangelist's mind then it might be expected that this 'fruitfulness' would refer to the showing of 'justice and righteousness' (Isaiah Ch. 5v7). However the **emphasis** in John's Gospel **is upon 'love'**, as the basis of the relationship of the Father and the Son; this quality of love is also shown by Jesus to his disciples. It is in this love of Christ that they are called upon to abide; they are to be rooted in Christ. Yet again there is challenge in Jesus' words as to abide in his love they are to **keep his commandments**, for it is through Jesus keeping his Father's commandments that he abides in his love. Jesus does not utter these words as a threat but as words of joy and opportunity to enable 'your joy may be full' (v11).

In v12 the essence of Jesus' commandments is indicated; it is none other than **loving one another. Thus the 'principle is agape'** (Dodd, pg412). Yet again there is challenge, for the love they are called on to demonstrate is to be love as Jesus himself has demonstrated. In v13 there is also the indication that Jesus is to 'lay down his life for his friends' which no 'greater love' can be shown. This love of Jesus becomes the 'standard of love' (Beasley-Murray, pg274) demanded of his followers who can thereby truly be his friends and therefore be saved by his atoning sacrifice, but this has itself to be earned by obedience to him. Such keeping of Jesus' commands instead of showing their inferiority as servants actually is the way to elevate the disciples to a position of 'friend'. The stress is not then on Jesus as a lord commanding servants but on a **new relationship** side by side with Jesus as they have had revealed to them everything Jesus has heard from his Father. Thus, there is an **intimacy** indicated between Jesus and the disciples which also opens the channels of supplication with the Father so they might receive all that they ask in Jesus' name.

In v16 it is clearly stated that the disciples are there with Jesus on his initiative not by their choice, seen by many as a possible indication of predeterminism. It also hints at the privilege which is theirs, though again their 'ordination' is to go forward and achieve the bringing forth of fruit that 'remains'. To emphasise the point they are again commanded (v17) to love one another, for it is this fruitful love that unites them with Vine Jesus and which in turn enables them to remain fruitful. While Barclay notes (pg274) that in **Rabbinic literature** the 'vine becomes the picture of the restored Israel, perhaps John saw this united fruitful Christian community fulfilling yet replacing this 'picture'. Perhaps too he would look forward to how the **Christian New Israel** would also fulfil the Rabbinic saying quoted by Barclay (pg275), "As the vine is the least of all the trees, and yet is the master of all, so the people of Israel appear insignificant in the world, but in the future (that is, in the messianic age) their soverignty will extend from one end of the world to the other."

The True Vine discourse has been suggested by many as having sacramental overtones and linked with the **Eucharist**. Thus, Marsh (pg521) sees both chapters 6 and 15 as containing 'profound eucharistic theology', while Barrett (pg470) indicates that if chapter 15 is in the context of the 'supper' then this would support that the symbolism of the vine is 'in part eucharistic'. These observations may be determined by the link, albeit to some tenuous, of the vine producing grapes which could in turn produce the wine elsewhere linked with Jesus' blood. Jesus would then be the source of the wine (blood) later depicted by the evangelist as flowing from the side of Jesus when he was on the cross. It may be that the wine-giving grapes grown by the disciple branches, which grew because they were united in the vine, would illustrate that to 'remain' truly in the love of Christ necessitated participation in the Eucharist.

▶**Additional material** (15v18-Ch. 16v4)

The grapes produced by the disciple branches might also suggest that the wine/blood was not merely that of Jesus but of his followers too; for as Christian crop-producers they will be separated from and hated by the world (v18) for Jesus has chosen his followers out of the world (v19), and in v20 '**If they have persecuted me, they will also persecute you**'. Jesus is emphasising that such persecution is not a vague possibility for they as his followers must themselves expect such a destiny; for it is to become (and indeed may have become by the time of the evangelist) the hallmark of a first-century Christian. The words of 11 Baruch 36-39, where the vine as messiah is the source for a fountain flowing to destroy the forest of trees symbolic of the enemies of God, might offer consolation and encouragement if they were recalled. The role of suffering is to be that of the disciples, yet 'celebrated' and foreshadowed in the very act of participating in the Eucharist.

While it will not lessen their suffering, disciples, whenever they existed, might be appreciative of Jesus' comments that the world's opposition is described as sin. Jesus had both spoken to and performed his unique works among them and yet the world's response was to hate Jesus , which for the evangelist (v23), is also to hate the Father. Such hatred was also to fulfil scripture (probably Psalm 69, though also possibly Psalm 35) 'They hated me without a cause'. For Grayston (Pg133) **this is their sin**, not that they were disobedient to the God they worshipped and defended, but **that they refused** or were unable to listen to or perceive **the Father's new initiative in his son Jesus**.

To further **encourage his followers in their persecution**, Jesus (v26ff) reintroduces the **Paraclete**, who, while he is to testify to Jesus, may also be assumed to 'comfort' them in their distress. Yet they still have a role to perform, also to bear witness to Jesus as they have been with him from the beginning (v27).

Indications of suffering continue in chapter 16v1-4. Jesus' intention is to ensure they appreciate the forewarning he is giving them so as to encourage them to **persevere**. Nor does Jesus 'pull any punches' as he reveals they will both be **excommunicated from Jewish synagogues and even killed**. While it may be ironical that their Jewish persecutors believe they are serving God in attacking Jesus' followers, such persecution will nevertheless be real.

NON 'I AM SAYINGS' DISCOURSES

▶**Nicodemus Discourse** (Ch. 3v1-21)

It is acknowledged that this passage is a discourse (eg. Barrett pg131, Dodd pg303) which contains a **minimum of narrative** (Barrett, pg 202). The discourse is perhaps best described as **dramatic dialogue** which **moves into monologue**, a feature that is characteristic of the Fourth Gospel. It is also generally observed that the 'monologue' of Jesus itself possibly develops from v16 into the **evangelist's own reflections**.

The character Nicodemus acting as an interlocutor, has in fact little to say; his contribution amounts only to four sentences, and he disappears from the discourse as it proceeds, seemingly forgotten as the monologue develops.

Yet the part that Nicodemus plays is of significance. He is described as a ruler of the Jews belonging to the Pharisaic party. He approaches Jesus, but '**by night**', which is often suggested as indicating the state of Nicodemus **within the 'darkness' of the world** rather than a mere historical observation. Scholars reflect on that 'darkness' with suggestions that it may represent a lack of moral and spiritual insight (Carson, pg186) or merely being in the dark about just who Jesus is. Similarly some have suggested that Nicodemus may not have been a real historical figure but is a **'created' representative of the Jews and Judaism** which Marsh suggests is 'at its best' (pg173) yet still inadequate (pg176).

However, it is to be remembered that Nicodemus **does actually come to Jesus**, perhaps searching for something. He acknowledges Jesus to be a rabbi, a teacher and one whose signs show him to be from God. Jesus' response is to indicate that to see the kingdom of God one needs to be born 'anew'. The word for **'anew', ('anothen' in Greek)** means both **'again'** and **'from above'**. Jesus or the evangelist may intend both meanings in that a new birth is necessary and that it must be a spiritual/heavenly renewal perhaps rendered by the one who himself is from above. In typical Johannine fashion, the unenlightened Nicodemus **misunderstands** and is unable to grasp the spirituality of Jesus' words asking 'physically', 'How can a man be born when he is old? Can he enter a second time into his mother's womb and be born?', yet to be fair to Nicodemus, as Marsh observes, this comment seems deliberately ambiguous (pg175).

Yet such misunderstandings enable the teaching within the discourse to advance further. So Jesus' use of **'pneuma'** in 3v8 may also be a play on words for it can mean **wind** which may 'blow' or **the Spirit**, but allows Jesus to indicate that to actually become part of God's rule it is necessary to be born both of water and spirit, which some see as indicating both water and spiritual baptism. Thus mere water purification carried out by the Jews, or even the water baptism of the Essenes, is not sufficient; to gain salvation perhaps **Christian baptism** and Jesus' **breathed spirit is necessary**. Bultmann (pg138-9) has suggested that 'water and' has been added to 'spirit' by a redactor in order for the church to portray Christian baptism being endorsed by Jesus.

Nicodemus himself must be born anew and born of the spirit. A marked **contrast** is also indicated **between the spirit and the flesh**, the former state at present seemingly eluding Nicodemus, for with lack of insight he interjects, "How can this be?" (v10). From this point Nicodemus takes no further part in the discourse as Jesus' teaching in recorded **in monologue form**, in what (Sanders and Mastin pg129) is a 'meditation inspired by the conversation...and developing out of it'.

There seems again accusation that the witness and testimony of the 'we' in v11 is not received. (Some have again seen the 'we' to refer to the early church (Johannine) rather than merely referring possibly to Jesus and his disciples). Clearly spiritual appreciation is beyond those who are unbelieving even of the earthly revelations.

It has already been established through the words of Nicodemus that Jesus was a rabbi, a teacher and one sent by God to perform 'signs'. Yet in this later part of the discourse the evangelist reflects on the more spectacular identification of **Jesus as son of man and Son of God**. The heavenly origin of Jesus as son of man is announced, though Jesus has descended from heaven. He has come so that those who believe in him may have eternal life. To achieve this he is to be 'lifted up', generally interpreted as crucified on the cross; similarly some have interpreted a link with Jesus and the snake lifted up by Moses in the wilderness which gave life to all who looked upon it (Nums. Ch. 21v49).

In v16-21 the evangelist's **focus falls on salvation**. He indicates that God, because he loved the world, sent Jesus to enable the believer to receive salvation and avoid **judgement** and condemnation. Moreover, this salvation, rather than being enjoyed at the end of the world, may be **immediately realised** by those believing. Yet a choice still has to be made between believing and choosing to remain in the dark. For while Jesus is identified as the 'only Son of God' and the 'light', the dark unbelievers avoid his presence because they do not wish their evil to be illuminated. The one who does what is true in contrast comes to the light (v21).

Nicodemus may have shown himself ignorant of the spiritual intention within Jesus' message yet he had approached the 'light' Jesus and so may at least be outside the 'evil' circle. Indeed it may be that his later (**Ch. 7v51**) comment to the Sanhedrin that Jesus ought to be given a fair hearing before he is condemned, and his coming with the disciple Joseph of Arimathea to bury Jesus (**Ch. 19v38-42**) indicate that he has been further enlightened to become himself a believing son of light. However, the other Pharisees it may be supposed in remaining unenlightened and opponents of Jesus (even it seems in 8v52 of Nicodemus as well), have chosen the darkness of 'condemnation'.

▶ **Samaritan woman discourse** (Ch. 4v1-42)

The evangelist sets the scene for the ensuing discourse through some descriptive material in which he states that Jesus' disciples were having more success with baptisms than John the Baptist. The evangelist in an apparent aside indicates that Jesus was not actually himself baptising. This may be to separate Jesus from mere water baptism as he is to be the **baptiser with the Holy Spirit**. Yet this observation by the evangelist may also link this discourse with the Nicodemus discourse. In the latter discourse Jesus had emphasised the need for such spiritual baptism and in this Samaritan woman discourse **'living water'** (in Ch. 7v39 identified with the Spirit) is considered.

John also mentions how, when the Pharisees discovered Jesus' greater success than that of John the Baptist, Jesus decided to go to Galilee; there seems more than a hint here of Jesus **needing to avoid potential Pharisaic hostility** in Judea. It should be noted that while in the Synoptic Gospels Galilee is the apparent centre of Pharisaic opposition to Jesus in the Fourth Gospel it is a place of 'support'. So Jesus journeyed towards Galilee, passing through Samaria on his way there. Another route would normally have been taken by Jews for they would have wished to avoid Samaria. Yet Jesus **deliberately chose to travel through Samaritan territory**; perhaps he (and the evangelist) are suggesting a movement away from the Pharisees and Judaism towards gentiles.

Jesus sat down by Jacob's well at Sychar apparently weary from the journey there. A Samaritan woman comes to the well to obtain water. The **timing of her coming** is unexpected as it would have been at a time when it would have been hot and which would have been avoided for such work. This has led to suggestions that she had deliberately chosen such a time to avoid meeting any other women because she was possibly shunned or despised because of her **apparent immoral life** indicated later in the discourse. If this supposition is correct then it makes even more poignant that Jesus a Jewish male, whose disciples have gone into town to buy food, speaks to her a foreign woman, one in shame and isolation. He **does not avoid her nor despise her** though, as is shown in v18, he knows of her past. Instead he asks her for a drink and a **dialogue ensues between them**. She is surprised he speaks to her and seems to be asking to use her vessel when as the evangelist explains Jews and Samaritans would not share drinking vessels.

Indeed the evangelist seems to use the Samaritan woman to further his theology.

When Jesus states that if she knew who Jesus was and what God was offering as a gift she would have asked Jesus for water that was 'living', as Nicodemus before her, she only seems to have the capacity to **see things in an earthly 'natural' way**. She wonders both how Jesus can give her water when he has no bucket and the well is deep and from where he gets this 'living water'. She further wonders, with characteristic irony (Barrett pg234), **if he is greater than their claimed ancestor Jacob** who used the well and gave it to the Samaritans, and taking Jesus' words literally she seeks his water merely to avoid having to journey to the well rather than appreciating Jesus is revealing spiritual truths to her.

Her statement that she has no husband while being true does not tell the whole truth for she has had 5 husbands and is now living with someone out of wedlock. When Jesus shows he is aware of this the **woman herself shows some perception** in concluding that Jesus must be a prophet; previously she had called him a Jew (v9), though had more respectfully called him 'sir' in v11. Following some teaching of Jesus and his statement that he is the Christ, she journeys to tell the Samaritan villagers about Jesus, **acting almost like a witness to Jesus**. She seems herself enlightened and goes to bring others to the light.

Yet, while John may focus on the woman as a possible 'example', it is **on Jesus that in reality the spotlight falls**. Throughout the discourse the evangelist reveals both the nature of Jesus and his teaching. In v1-6 it is implied that Jesus' greater success shows he is **superior to John the Baptist**; this may have been of particular significance to the Johannine church if, as some suggest, there was some competing John the Baptist sect in its area. Similarly, a **contrast** is made **between the water of Jacob's well**, which 'whoever drinks will thirst again', and that **living water of Jesus** which will permanently quench the thirst and 'will become in him a spring of water welling up to eternal life'. This seems to answer in the affirmative the woman's question, 'Are you greater than our father Jacob?'

However, the evangelist may also wish to show something other than the greatness of Jesus. In v6 it is recorded how 'Jesus wearied as he was with his journey, sat down beside the well'. Some, especially those who see the Gospel as anti-gnostic, or more particularly as anti-Docetic, have identified this as the evangelist's touch designed to **'emphasise Jesus' humanity'** (Barrett pg231) and counteract such groups. However, it may be, together with the statement that it was 'about the sixth hour' (that is noon), that John is merely presenting a 'historical' indication.

The evangelist also shows that Jesus, in being aware that the woman has had 5 husbands and is now living with someone out of wedlock, seems to be a prophet as he acts like a **'seer' of old**. This **'knowingness'** on the part of Jesus is often demonstrated (eg. Ch. 1v48; 2v25; 5v6; 11v14). Yet for the evangelist Jesus is more than some 'knowing' prophet. Thus, when the woman seeks Jesus' opinion on the true place people ought to worship, the Jewish Jerusalem or on the Samaritan Mount Gerizim, where their temple had stood before it was destroyed by the Jew John Hyrcanus, Jesus becomes an authoritative teacher and **enlightener**. His reply seems to indicate that the real issue should not centre on the 'where' of worship but on its nature. **True worship** it seems is that which is based on spirit and truth, and 'the hour is coming, and now is' (v23) when true worshippers will fulfil this requirement of God. As for the evangelist's community Jesus is both the new temple (Ch. 2v21) from which flows the waters of life (perhaps an echo of Ezekiel Ch. 47v1ff) and the 'Truth', it may be implied that true worship and salvation (which is from the Jews v22) is revealed by Jesus; for the Johannine church, 'we worship what we know.' It may also be that there is a call not to concentrate on old issues that have divided people but to **concentrate on the unifying nature of Jesus**.

The woman reveals she is aware that the coming messiah will reveal all these things. However, the true 'revealer' is before her. She has awaited his coming but needs to be told he is actually there. Jesus **states that he is the messiah**, 'I who speak to you am he.' The **'I am' here** is taken by most not to be theologically loaded (Carson pg227) but merely to be an indication of something like 'the messiah, it is none other than I'. This is how the woman interprets Jesus' words as she speedily goes to tell fellow Samaritans that they should come to see themselves one who has shown himself to be the revealer of 'all that I ever did'. She asks the question, though acting in an almost missionary capacity as she seems to believe it herself, **'Can this be the Christ?'**

Indeed her 'testimony' persuades many of the Samaritans to believe in Christ. Though after he stays with them for two days many more believed because they had experienced his presence themselves; they no longer believed because of the woman's words but because 'we have heard for ourselves, and we know that this is indeed the **Saviour of the world**' (v42); Jesus is the universal saviour. What a marked contrast there is here with the Lucan Ch.9v51ff where the Samaritan villagers refuse to receive Jesus which incites the brothers James and John to want God to destroy them with fire from heaven.

Such a **harvest of believers** had been indicated by Jesus to the returning disciples in the discourse material of v31-38. Their conversation seemed to act as another vehicle for Jesus' teaching. When they encouraged him to physically eat, he tried to focus their attention on his food being 'to do the will' of his Father; also he wants them to appreciate that while there was still four months until the time of the 'physical' harvest the time of the spiritual harvest of souls was already there. This harvest of Samaritan believers was to be theirs though others had worked to bring it about; not least perhaps the Samaritan woman.

A final comment needs to be made on **symbolism** possibilities within the discourse. For example Jesus' words above about **'harvest'** are almost universally interpreted as referring to the gathering in of the souls of Christian believers, in this instance seemingly those of the Samaritan villagers. Yet even references such as **Jesus sitting wearied at the well** may be a painted picture of the evangelist to indicate (as suggested above) Jesus' humanity rather than an actual description of an action of Jesus.

Clearly, many may argue that the descriptions are in fact to be taken as historical. Thus the **'sixth hour'** in v6 may merely be an eyewitness recollection of what time it was; though in this case the eyewitness has to be either Jesus himself or the woman for no one else is present with them. Others have accepted that it may be a way that the evangelist can heighten the degradation of the woman who has to come in the heat of the day. Yet it has also been pointed out that Jesus was crucified after the sixth hour in John, so the reference in chapter 4, when Jesus' humanity is also suggested, may be a foreshadowing of the sacrifice of his human body on the cross. It might also be noted that Jesus meets the woman when it is most light perhaps to contrast with the previous meeting with Nicodemus which was at night.

Some have also suggested that the references to the **woman's husbands and lover** may be linked to **Samaritan worship**, indicating the gods worshipped by the Samaritans, and possibly a reference influenced by 2 Kings Ch. 17v30-32. However, some scholars do believe that the evangelist would not "allegorise in this manner" (Beasley-Murray, pg 61); he also points out that in the 2 Kings reference 7 gods not 5 are mentioned. In fact the 5 husbands plus the 'lover' would make 6. No doubt Beasley-Murray, and those almost dismissing symbolism, would be horrified at the suggestion that there are 6 in John for the very reason that Samaritan worship is short of that 'perfection' of 7 (as may also be the 6 Jewish waterpots in Ch. 2v6). Perhaps Jesus is himself to be seen as that 'seventh'. Moreover, immediately after the mention of the husbands and lover in John Jesus begins to teach the woman about true 'worship'.

Finally, it has been suggested that the woman **leaving her water jar** and then going to tell others about Jesus is possibly symbolic. It is generally suggested it may mean she is leaving her old life behind. Also she may have realised that she does not need the jar as Jesus has living water for her. (Note symbolism has been dealt with here at some length to aid appreciation and to indicate areas of debate on the issue).

▶ **Discourse after the Healing of the Crippled man** (Ch. 5v19-47)

The evangelist records in v16 that the Jews persecuted Jesus for healing on the Sabbath. But Jesus upsets the Jews even further by stating (v17), 'My Father is working still, and I am working.' which to them was blasphemy as Jesus was in effect making himself equal to God. **The miracle 'sets in motion a long discourse'** (Barrett pg13) in which a 'case' seems to be made for the **special relationship that Jesus has with the Father and the role of the Son**. Certain **'witnesses'** are cited in support of Jesus' claims, and the Jews themselves are placed under the 'accusation' of Moses at the close of the discourse. The passage seems reminiscent of a court case where, here in particular, the **case for the defence** of Jesus is indicated. The substance of that defence is what the world is called upon to believe about the person of Jesus in order to gain life.

The whole passage v19-47 is recorded as a **monologue** of Jesus **without interruption** from any within his audience. Marsh notes (pg259) that the 'truly, truly' of v19 is a solemn formula which often seems to mark the transition into monologue, and further (pg260/1) he shows how while other commentators have seen the passage as a transition from miracle to discourse he believes that "the narrative of the miracle and the exposition of the discourse are really a profound unity". While that may be so, Barrett suggests (pg257) that the discourse can be divided into three sections; v19-30 dealing with the dependence and unity of the Father and Son, v31-40 about witness, and v41-47 concerned with unbelief. The following comments will be made using thése three divisions.

Verses 19-30—Barrett (pg260) sees **parallelism of the Son and Father** as the keynote of this passage. Initially, v19, Jesus indicates that he is aware of the actions of the Father and acts in unison with him performing the same deeds. The Son acts according to the will of the Father. Their unity is based on love. The Father will reveal to the Son 'greater works' so that the people will 'marvel'. There seems an indication that this will involve the **Son raising the dead and giving them life** just as the Father does. This will be fulfilled 'literally' later in the raising of Lazarus. Further the role of **judgement** is passed by the Father to the Son. The discourse seems to encourage honouring the Son, listening to his message and believing, for this is the key to possessing eternal life; it will enable the believer to avoid judgement. This is the proclamation of the Gospel.

The **emphasis is on life**. Even the dead, seemingly both those physically and spiritually dead, will come to live because of the Son; he has been granted the power of giving life but also authority to execute judgement because he is Son of man. The resurrection to life for the good and the resurrection to judgement for the evil is both 'coming' and 'now is'. Thus **future and realised eschatology are fused** in the activity of the Son. He judges justly as he acts with the authority and by the will of the Father (v30) which is the conclusion to the discourse as it was its beginning in v19.

The next section, **v31-40**, is concerned essentially with the **theme of witness**. Jesus' message so far may have merely upset the traditionalists within the audience even more as they would conclude Jesus was continuing to claim a relationship with the Father that was blasphemous. Further, Jesus was bearing witness about himself and so according to Jewish law was not speaking the 'truth'. (This echoes the Jews accusation in chapter 8v13 discussed above). What hostility and doubting of his claims there is seems handled without delay as Jesus testifies to his co-witnesses. Dodd remarks (pg330) that there is here 'Christian evidences' in which 'we can hardly be wrong in finding a reflection of the practice of missionary apologetics in the early church.'

Four **'big guns' witnesses** are cited in support of Jesus. The first is **John the Baptist** whom Jesus states 'has borne witness to the truth'. Yet Jesus is keen to indicate that his other witnesses are more impressive than the testimony of a 'man'. The second and 'greater' testimony is the **'works'** which he performs, granted by the Father for Jesus to accomplish. The Greek for 'works' is 'erga' which is acknowledged as being Jesus own word for the 'signs' (semeia). These erga are evidence that Jesus has indeed been sent by the Father. It is **the Father himself** who is Jesus' third witness. However, the people have no knowledge of the Father's voice, form, or word and so do not believe on the one 'sent'. The final witness cited in this discourse is **'the scriptures'**. Ironically the Jews believe that they have eternal life through the scriptures, yet as they ignore their witness and do not come to Christ they will in fact not receive life.

According to Barrett the third section in the discourse is **v41-47** and is about **unbelief**. While in fact many times already from v24 the need to believe in the one sent by the Father has been mentioned; from v41 the consequences of unbelief for the Jews is spelled out. They are criticised not only for rejecting the one sent by the Father from the heavenly sphere but because they are willing to accept apparent earthly claimants. Some scholars have suggested there may here be a reference not merely to some generalisation about false messianic claimants but about the rebel Bar Cochba in particular. This is clearly an assumption, though possibly with some substance; if so it would indicate that at least this part of the gospel was written after 132 CE the date of Bar Cochba's revolt.

The final irony is that the **Jews are to face accusation themselves from Moses** the one whom they would have expected to be on their side in prosecuting Jesus for breaking the Sabbath and blaspheming. The impression given is that Moses is in fact on Jesus' side, perhaps another witness for the defence. They have not believed Moses' scriptural words about Jesus so neither will they believe the words of Jesus himself. Thus Moses also becomes a witness for the prosecution, not of Jesus, but of the unbelieving Jews.

▶ **The Tabernacles' discourse** (Ch. 7v1-39)

These verses seem to contain some **rather fragmentary material**. Dodd suggests (pg345) that the chapter, together with chapter 8, bear the appearance of being a collection of **miscellaneous material** in what may be produced as a series of **controversial dialogues**, possibly unconnected, and at least having no long continuous discourse presentation. While this may be true, the evangelist has brought the possible separate sections together. His reason may be because they all seem connected with **opinions about Jesus**, particularly (repeatedly) indicating that Jesus had his **supporters** as well as **opponents**, and showing how the accusations of those opponents were answered by Jesus (or are answered by the Johannine church). Indeed the sections will be considered around possible questions about Jesus and Christianity that might have needed answering.

In v1-9 the question under focus appears to be **why Jesus worked in Galilee almost in secret** rather than openly revealing himself to the whole world. In answer the evangelist shows how the life of Jesus is threatened. Initially John comments how Jesus has been forced to stay in Galilee avoiding Judea as the "**Jews sought to kill him**". Even Jesus' own brothers seem to incite him to go to Judea to reveal himself to the world rather than 'work in secret'. There appears the possibility of **animosity from the brothers** to Jesus or at least (v5) a lack of belief in him, literally fulfilling Ch. 1v11 "He came to his own home, and his **own people received him not**". He replies that his time has not yet come (v6) or 'fully' come (v8). This time or '**hour**' in John's Gospel is generally interpreted as referring to Jesus **crucifixion**. This is hinted at in v7 with the reference to the world hating Jesus because Jesus testifies against its evil works. Jesus states the world does not oppose his brothers who should themselves go to Jerusalem; yet refusing to be goaded into an open messianic revelation he himself is "not going up to this feast" of Tabernacles.

Verses **10-13**—It seems strange that Jesus did in fact go to Jerusalem for the feast but still in keeping with what he had said he went 'in private'. The Jews are seeking Jesus and John clearly indicates, as he often does, that there is a **division of opinion** about Jesus; he has his supporters who think "he is a good man", and his opponents who believe "he is leading the people astray".

Verses 14-18—The focus of this section is on **how Jesus has 'learning when he has never studied'**. The answer to this is that Jesus' **teaching is that of the Father**; Jesus is not merely acting on his own authority as that might imply he was seeking his own glory whereas in fact Jesus is seeking the glory of the Father; this shows Jesus is 'true, and in him there is no falsehood'.

Verses 19-24—This section seems to have no real connection with the previous material but seems to **debate points about the law**. In v19 Jesus accuses his listeners of not keeping the Mosaic law as they **seek to kill him**. They in turn retort that he must be mad as 'Who is seeking to kill you?' In what seems a reference back to the healing of the crippled man which he had performed on the Sabbath he states he performed a deed at which they marvelled. He also seems to tease them by referring to how **circumcision takes priority over Sabbath law** according to Mosaic law, so if part of a man's body can be operated on the Sabbath why should they oppose him for making 'a man's whole body well?' (v23). He seems to be scolding them for **judging by appearances**.

Verses 25-31—In this section **Jesus' messiahship seems debated**. Some people wonder if the authorities believe Jesus to be the messiah as they had wanted to kill him yet he now speaks openly without opposition. Others retort that Jesus cannot be the messiah as they know where he comes from whereas no one will know the origins of the messiah. Again there may be irony here for they are only judging by those 'appearances' of his earthly background. Again to indicate the **closeness of Jesus and the Father**, Jesus, while admitting they may know him and where he comes from, states they do not appreciate he has been sent by the Father whom they do not know. Jesus claims knowledge of the Father as his origins are with him. The evangelist records that for this some sought to arrest him but others believed in him seemingly as the messiah who would do no more signs than Jesus has performed.

Verses 32-36—(In v32 the evangelist indicates that the chief priests and Pharisees sent officers to arrest Jesus). This section centres on the **question of Jesus' 'going'**. Jesus teaches that in a short while he is to return to the Father who sent him, and that they will not find him or accompany him. This causes the Jews to wonder about his destination misguidedly thinking he may intend to go to 'the Dispersion among the Greeks' to teach them. There may also be irony here if the 'destination' of John's Gospel was to such a 'dispersed' group rather than to Palestinian Jews.

Verses 37-39—Jesus invites the **thirsty to come to him to drink**. He speaks on the last day of the feast of Tabernacles when the 'water libations' took place. The evangelist may intend Jesus' **'living water'** to replace the physical libations for his water will flow within them with spiritual force in fulfilment of scripture. The evangelist interprets 'living water' in v39 as the **Spirit** which will be given when Jesus has been glorified. Thus the question of Jesus' relationship with the spirit is partially answered to be enumerated upon later by the evangelist particularly within the Paraclete passages.

▶**The discourse when 'Greeks' arrive** (Ch. 12v20-50)

For Beasley-Murray (pg207) the "function of the discourse is to show **the necessity of the death and exaltation of Jesus** for the establishment of the saving soverignity of God that embraces **all nations**."

The desire of some Greeks to see Jesus signals the time for Jesus to announce the **arrival of his 'hour' of glorification**, which (Bultmann pg424) is at the same time his hour of 'passion'. In v24, in possible parabolic words, he indicates he needs to die to ensure 'growth' and fruitfulness. There is a hint that this dying is also to be a fate shared by his 'servants', yet for hating their earthly lives they will receive the prized eternal life. In v27 Jesus admits his 'soul is troubled', yet in what seems a **contrast to the Synoptics**' Gethsemane appeal (Mk Ch. 14v36 "Abba, Father... remove this cup from me"), he is not to ask the Father to save him from 'this hour' rather he wishes the Father's name to be glorified. God speaks (v28) 'I have glorified it, and I will glorify it again' namely when Jesus dies on the cross. The crowd do not appreciate that God has spoken even though Jesus says he has done so on their behalf.

Jesus indicates that both his hour and the **time of judgement for the world and its 'ruler' the devil** have arrived. In contrast Jesus will be 'lifted up' to enable 'all men' to be drawn to him and presumably to **universalistic salvation**. The crowd seem perplexed as they believe that the messiah will live for ever and so they question Jesus' being lifted up and who is the 'son of man' about whom he speaks. He tries to lead them to appreciating the need to walk in his light while he remains with them rather than to blindly walk in the darkness. However, as the evangelist indicates by reference to Isaiah Ch. 53v1 and Ch. 6v10, the people did not believe him, though in v42 the evangelist indicates that some, even of the authorities, believed in him though not openly for fear of **excommunication from the synagogue**. This may have been the actual fate of some within the Johannine community.

In v44-50 there is an implied last **appeal**, as this section marks the end of his public teaching, from Jesus **for belief**. He states that to believe and see him is also to see the one who sent him. Jesus as the light will bring the believer out of darkness. However, while Jesus has come to save rather than to judge, the one rejecting Jesus will in fact be judged by the word Jesus has spoken; Jesus is merely speaking the Father's words which in fact do give people the opportunity to gain eternal life. Barrett comments (pg434) that 'In Paul and John glorification and condemnation are opposite sides of the same process; to refuse the justifying love of God in Christ is to incur judgement.'

▶ **The final discourse** (Ch. 16v5-33)

Comments were made earlier about Ch. 16v1-4 in which Jesus indicated suffering would occur for his disciples. In this passage he concentrates on telling them **more about the Paraclete** and **his own going away** but within the context of **'joy'** rather than sorrow. Jesus appreciates that they are sorrowful because is going away, but he tries to reassure them that it is to be to their advantage as then the Paraclete (Holy Spirit) can be sent by him to them. He indicates that the **role of the Paraclete** will be to convince (or convict) the world 'concerning sin and righteousness and judgement'. Essentially he wishes to show that the world is condemned for refusing to believe in him and that his righteousness will be demonstrated by his return to the Father and the devil being judged. The Paraclete will also guide them 'into all the truth' acting like a prophetic revealer; he will also glorify Jesus (v12-15). (See 'Holy Spirit' booklet for more analysis).

In v16 he states that though in a little while they will see him no more yet in a little while and they will see him again. The **monologue** form of the discourse is briefly suspended at this point as the disciples talk over his words as they do not understand their meaning. **Jesus is aware** of their desire to ask him, 'perhaps John thought of spiritual discernment on the part of Jesus' (Barrett, pg492) and this typically allows Jesus to clarify his comment with the usual 'truly, truly' introduction. He indicates that they are to be sorrowful in the near future while in contrast the world will rejoice. However their sorrow will be turned to joy which Jesus illustrates by reference to the common Old Testament image of a woman in pain during childbirth but happy, and forgetting that pain, when her child is born. The basis for their **joy is because 'I will see you again'**, which some commentators see not only as his resurrection but also possibly as his parousia (Marsh, pg542).

In v23-28 Jesus explains how the disciples will be given whatever they ask of the Father as he loves them; there will even be no need for Jesus to mediate on their behalf. The disciples appear to appreciate, as he is 'speaking plainly and not in any figure', that he has come from and is returning to the Father. Yet even with such apparent believing the disciples are forewarned that **they will be scattered leaving him** though the Father will remain with him. Yet this comment of Jesus is not 'for condemnation but encouragement, for he anticipates their speedy recovery (Beasley-Murray, pg288) as this will not be their final destiny as he wants them to have peace; in the world there will be tribulation for them but they should appreciate that they will be joyous as he has **'overcome the world'**. Thus, this should produce the 'confidence of the Church' as it 'is based on Christ's victory' (Sanders and Mastin, pg367).

BRIEF COMMENTS ABOUT SOURCES, HISTORICITY AND PURPOSES OF THE DISCOURSES

The Scholar Bultmann has made the suggestion that the evangelist of the Fourth Gospel has used a **discourse-source** in producing his discourse material. This is a counterpart to his suggested 'sign-source'. Many scholars question his suggestions (though there seems more sympathy for the sign-source); it is thought he is too radical, particularly in suggesting the source is made up of **revelation speeches of some gnostic group**. These speeches have apparently been translated into Greek by the evangelist and set in a Christian and historical setting. **Scholars have sought other sources**; yet while Borgen and others believe John may have created some discourses as 'commentaries' on Jewish texts, this does not then necessarily lead them to conclude such material was already a 'collection' of textual expositions acquired, though altered, by the evangelist. Similarly, while John's Gospel may be linked with a diversity of 'background' material there is still considerable debate over whether he was influenced by that material. Carson (pg41-42) concludes that while "John no doubt used sources" they cannot necessarily be retrieved; also to many the **pursuit of separate sources would seem a "lost cause"**.

The question of the **historicity** of the gospel discourses is also debated; the crux of the debate is whether in the Johannine material the actual words of Jesus are retained. Clearly the suggestions of Form and Redaction critics this century, whether accepted or not, have called into question how much material in the gospels actually goes back to Jesus rather than to the early church or the evangelists themselves. Many who are sceptical over the Synoptic records of Jesus' teaching are even more **questioning over the long discourses** presented in the Fourth Gospel. Many see these as **sermonistic** and more the **literary constructions** of the evangelist rather than how Jesus addressed his audiences. However, there are those, particularly who follow the suggestion of a very early date for the Gospel, who believe that the discourses in John's Gospel better capture what would have been said in the hostile confrontations Jesus would have encountered and **may be more 'true' to Jesus'**

words than the Synoptics. Again there is no consensus on the matter; scholars like Borgen may see unity within the discourses but they do not see in them Jesus' words, while Hunter would argue there is no evidence to show that the material is not **authentic**. Some (e.g. Carson) would like to see early traditions behind the evangelist's Christian insights so that within the discourses Jesus' voice may still be heard.

In considering the possible **purpose/s** of the evangelist in his recording of the discourses it seems appropriate to listen to the evangelist's own words in Ch. 20v31, **"these are written that you may believe that Jesus is the Christ, the Son of God, and that believing you may have life in his name"** (though note that some suggest these are the words of the Johannine community or even some redactor). While these words are normally taken to refer to Jesus' 'signs' they may also reflect the evangelist's aim in the discourses, particularly when those signs and discourses seem closely connected. The focus of the discourses seems to be on **the person of Jesus**, particularly in the 'I am' sayings where Jesus is recorded as drawing attention to himself. Jesus is indeed shown by John to be son of man, messiah, and the unique Son of God. It is even possible in his portrayal of Jesus' close relationship with the Father and Spirit that the evangelist believes Jesus to be divine in the same way that God is divine. He certainly seems to make **Jesus superior** to all others. This in itself may be one of John's purposes. His **superiority to John the Baptist** would counter any claims from the Baptist's sect that John was the messiah; so too Jesus' **superiority over the Old Testament characters** of Abraham, Jacob, and particularly Moses, would aid the claim that Jesus has come to replace Judaism as it stood, and for the church by Christianity. John also seems keen to **counter Jewish attacks** on Jesus and Christianity. The presentation also concentrates on what Jesus can do; thus **his death** is spotlighted not merely as a historical act but as the means to giving **eternal life**. This gift is itself highlighted in the discourses but within the context of '**believing**'. For while eternal life is available '**now**' as the eschaton is already to be experienced, it can only be obtained through believing in Jesus; lack of such belief brings the consequence of '**judgement**'. Finally, while the matter is one of fierce debate, it may be that John presents within his discourses **sacramental material**, both of baptism and the Eucharist as a reflection that they need to be practised within the Christian community.

WORKSHEET

1. Briefly consider the term 'I am'.
2. Comment briefly on the 'I am' statements contained in the following verses in particular pointing out any difference of type or emphasis—Ch. 4v26; 6v35; 8v28; Ch. 11v25; 18v6.
3. Write a brief note on the meaning of 'discourses' when applied to the Fourth Gospel.
4. With reference to any 3 'I am' sayings, list what may be learned about the person of Jesus.
5. Do you think that there is any justification in suggesting that the writer of the Fourth Gospel was influenced by the Old Testament in his presentation of Jesus' 'I am' sayings? Give reasons.
6. Make brief comments on why you think the evangelist refers to Moses in the following verses—Ch. 3v14; 5v45-47; 6v32; 7v23; 9v28-9.
7. Do you think there is any justification in linking the following passages with the Eucharist? Give reasons.—Ch. 6v53-58; 15v1-6.
8. Make brief comments on the major Johannine features displayed in Jesus' conversations with (a) Nicodemus, (b) the Samaritan woman.
9. In what ways may John's 'discourses' be described as 'distinctive'?
10. Do you think John's accounts of Jesus' discourses are historical?
11. Briefly consider how the Johannine presentation of the teaching of Jesus in the form of 'discourses' may cause difficulties for the present day reader.
12. Consider the purposes of the Fourth Evangelist in using 'discourses'.

EXAM QUESTIONS

The reason why most people fail exams at A-level and above is because they write irrelevant information as opposed to inaccurate information. The plea of examiners is always "answer the question asked". However, students often regurgitate answers from questions set during their studies. Such 'model' answers are used irrespective of the slant or emphasis in the exam question.

It is important that answers are planned before embarking on an essay. Not only does this allow a student to arrange material in a logical order but this also serves as an 'early warning system' showing whether they have sufficient knowledge to fully answer the question.

One useful method to aid keeping to the required material is to highlight key words and phrases in the question.

The following questions test 'appreciation' of the key areas:-
    1. The Fourth Evangelist's presentation of the person of Jesus.
    2. Jewish 'background' material.
    3. Content and significance of certain discourses.

Q1. " 'I am the bread of life', 'I am the true vine'.
With reference to the above 'I am' sayings, consider how far they aid an understanding of the Fourth Evangelist's distinctive presentation of the person of Jesus."

Using the method of highlighting key words in the question and dealing with them:

INDICATIONS SHOWN ABOUT 'THE PERSON OF JESUS'.
eg. Bread—'real', messiah, greater than Moses, giver of eternal life, heavenly et al.
Vine—'real', Son, sustainer, loving, hated and persecuted, dying (Eucharist), et al.
HOW DOES THE EVANGELIST 'PRESENT' 'THE PERSON OF JESUS'?
eg. Are there any general trends, characteristics, emphases etc.?
HOW MAY THE 'PRESENTATION' BE 'DISTINCTIVE'?
eg. aspects typical of/peculiar to John, contrast with Synoptics, etc.

HOW FAR DO THE 2 SAYINGS 'AID' THIS 'PRESENTATION'?
note -'How far' really is also requiring an 'how far not' consideration.
eg. allow more appreciation of specifics/Johannine thrusts, yet other points not included but seen elsewhere (in John/other sources), degree of 'aiding', et al.

Q2. "With reference to the 'Good Shepherd' saying, (a) discuss its Jewish background', (b) consider its significance for the early church."

(a) INDICATION OF RELEVANT BACKGROUND MATERIAL
eg. God as shepherd (Ps. 23,77; Isaiah 40), Good shepherd/king (Ezek. 34), messianic shepherd (Ps. Sol.17), bad shepherds/rulers (Jer 23; Ezek. 34) et al.
DISCUSSION OF MATERIAL INDICATED
eg. closeness to John?, influence?, relevance?, aid understanding?, main background?
(b) INDICATION OF POINTS OF SIGNIFICANCE
eg. person of Jesus, unity, universal salvation, death/resurrection, sacrifice, love et al.
CONSIDERATION OF SIGNIFICANCE
eg. situation of early church, encouragement, clarifications re Jesus' death, guidance.

Q3. "Comment on Jesus' discourses with (a) Nicodemus, (b) the Samaritan woman."

Note 'comment' instruction allows great scope, yet try to critically appraise/examine.

(a) eg. pattern of discourse, Nicodemus' relevance, initial mention of Nicodemus, major themes (eg light, above, judgement etc), person of Jesus, Pneuma, baptism, et al.

(b) eg. Samaritan/Jewish relations, person of Jesus (eg. prophet, greater than Jacob, messiah, Saviour of world), living water, Samaritan woman, true worship, witness et al.

FURTHER READING

The following books are not exclusively about 'discourses' but deal with the subject in relevant sections which must be selected.

THE GOSPEL ACCORDING TO ST. JOHN—by C. K. BARRETT
(SPCK: First published 1955)
Readability *, Content # # # #.
A very scholarly contribution. Introductory comments included pgs 11-21. Other comments within commentary sections.

JOHN—By G. R. BEASLEY-MURRAY (Word Publishing: U.K. Edition 1991)
Readability * *, Content # # #.
Appropriate material is in the comment and explanation sections.

THE GOSPEL ACCORDING TO JOHN—By R. E. BROWN
(Anchor Bible: Published by Doubleday 1966 (Vol.1), 1970 (Vol.2))
Readability * * *, Content # # #.
Sensible, challenging general comments within commentary sections, and especially useful Appendix 1V: Ego eimi—I am (Vol.1)

THE GOSPEL OF JOHN—By R. BULTMANN
(Blackwell: Translated by G.R. Beasley-Murray 1971)
Readability *, Content # # #.
General (sometimes radical) comments within the commentary sections.

THE GOSPEL ACCORDING TO JOHN—By D. A. CARSON
(IVP: First published 1991)
Readability * * *, Content # # #.
A fairly recent commentary in which the author considers the thinking of many scholars both on broad issues and particular points.

THE INTERPRETATION OF THE FOURTH GOSPEL—By C.H.DODD
(Cambridge University Press: First published 1953)
Readability * *, Content # # #.
Relevant material presented within the commentary sections.

THE GOSPEL OF JOHN—By K. GRAYSTON (Epworth: 1990)
Readability * * * *, Content # # #.
General useful comments in introductory pgs. xvii—xxv. 'I am' considered on pgs 61-62. Other relevant material in commentary sections.

ST. JOHN—By J. MARSH (Pelican: First published 1968)
Readability * * *, Content ####.
General comments pgs. 66-71 (1988 edition), and other scholarly comments given in commentary sections.

THE GOSPEL ACCORDING TO ST. JOHN—By R. SCHNACKENBURG (Burns & Oates: 1968 (Vol.1), 1980 (Vol.2), 1982 (Vol.3))
Readability * *, Content # # #.
Some sound general comments within the commentary sections. Particularly thorough on background considerations. Very useful section (Excursus 8. Vol.2) on 'The origin and meaning of ego eimi'

JOHN: EVANGELIST AND INTERPRETER—By S. SMALLEY (Paternoster:1978) Readability * * * , Content # # #.
Many interesting ideas presented in a very readable manner. Thoughtful consideration of the relationship between discourses and signs from page 88.

KEY	Readability	* manageable;	** good;
		*** very good;	**** excellent.
	Content	# adequate;	## good;
		### very good;	#### excellent.